BUILDING PROJECTS

HAMLYN PRACTICAL DIY GUIDES

BUILDING PROJECTS

John McGowan & Roger DuBern

HAMLYN

ACKNOWLEDGMENTS

Copy editor:
John Stace

Technical consultant:
Mike Trier

Art editor:
Lee Griffiths

Design:
Crucial Books

Special photography:
Jon Bouchier

Illustration:
Oxford Illustrators Limited

Picture research:
**Rachel Duffield, Frances Topp,
Julia Pashley**

Production controller:
Helen Seccombe

This edition published in 1990 by
The Hamlyn Publishing Group Limited
a division of
The Octopus Publishing Group
Michelin House
81 Fulham Road
LONDON SW3 6RB

ISBN 0-600-56589-0

Produced by Mandarin Offset
Printed and bound in Hong Kong

**The publishers wish to thank the
following organisations and
photographers for their kind permission
to reproduce the following pictures in
this book:**
Acme 46; Armitage Shanks 60b; Belle
Engineering 12r; Burmah/Solignum
13br; Edson Evers 52b; EEC Bradstone
52tl, 72/Quarries Ltd 80t; Errut 13tr;
Esco 13bl; GKN Kwikform Ltd 12t&c;
Houses & Interiors 34, 41, 49, 52tr;
Kango Ltd 13tl; Kew Hobby Ltd 13c;

MFI 60t; Tania Midgley 74, 77; Rentokil
69; Jessica Strang 42, 80l; Elizabeth
Whiting & Associates 59t, 74t, 77.

The following photographs were
specially taken for the Octopus
Publishing Group Picture Library:
Jon Bouchier 8–9, 10, 11, 14–15, 16–17,
18, 19.

All subjects for special photography
supplied by Sainsbury's Homebase.

CONTENTS

INTRODUCTION

Modern tools and materials have made it possible for every householder to become an expert do-it-yourselfer. No longer is it essential to employ a tradesman to repair, maintain and improve your home (assuming, of course, that you could find a good one who would charge you a reasonable price for the work).

Nowadays, power tools, man-made boards, modern adhesives, easy-to-use fixings and so on make it possible to take on a whole host of jobs that were once considered well out of the scope of the ordinary person.

All you need now is basic ability coupled with a sensible approach to a job. It has been said that successful DIY is comprised of 50% planning and 50% doing. This means thinking really carefully about the job in advance. You have to know or get good advice on the tools and equipment needed, the correct materials to use, the order in which to do things, and so on. Every home improvement job will be satisfying and rewarding if you approach it with patience. Always overestimate the time it will take you to do a job – there is nothing worse than thinking you can complete a project on Saturday morning and finding you are only halfway through by Sunday evening. The one thing that a do-it-yourselfer gets for nothing is time: so don't rush anything. Snags are bound to crop up from time to time; when they do, stop and think carefully how to sort them out. Never try to cut corners – it invariably causes more problems and wasted time later.

Both in planning and in working take the obvious, sensible precautions. Be confident that you know what you are doing: if you have any doubts, either before or during the work, call in an expert. This is especially important if the job entails plumbing, gas or electrical installation, or if alterations are to be made to loadbearing structures such as beams, rafters or brick walls.

Similarly, however experienced you are with machinery and equipment, do not disregard safety instructions. Switch off and unplug when it says so, and if gloves, mask or goggles are required, wear them.

Remember that your home is a huge investment. Improve it, add to it, maintain it, replan it and you will both enjoy it and reap financial rewards from it.

The range of projects in this book has been specially selected to cover all abilities. There are jobs for the beginner and more experienced alike.

Armed with the information, help, advice (plus lots of handy tips that are contained throughout) you can lay a patio, build a barbecue, install a new fireplace, construct fitted wardrobes – even make two rooms into one. Once you get started, you will amaze yourself with what you can achieve and be delighted with the results.

TOOLS

Every home owner needs a good, basic tool kit: both to improve the property and to handle routine maintenance or repairs.

Carefully chosen and looked after, a selection of good-quality tools will save you no end of money and inconvenience and will give a lifetime's service. A good tool kit is one of the best investments you will ever make.

You do not need to buy many tools to start with – additions can be made if and when needed and when you can afford to buy them. Never buy expensive specialist tools that may be needed only once in a blue moon – it is better to hire these, if you cannot borrow them.

Generally speaking, the best is your best bet. If, for example, you buy the cheapest possible set of screwdrivers, you will probably find they are bent and useless after a little pressure has been applied.

It does not usually pay to buy a ready-assembled tool kit in a nice wooden box.

Requirement number one is some power tools. Although you can get power assistance for virtually every job, the two basics are a drill and a jigsaw.

An ideal drill will have 13mm (½in) chuck, variable speed control and hammer action, so you can tackle a wide range of drilling jobs in all sorts of materials. If you will be drilling large holes in wood, you really need a hand-drill or a brace, and a selection of bits.

Buy high-speed steel twist drills for making holes in wood, plus two or three masonry drills for making holes in walls. Twist drills are sized in millimetres or in fractions of an inch. Masonry drills are sized by numbers that match screw gauges, or in millimetres.

A jigsaw can cut straight lines, curves and intricate shapes. You just fit the appropriate saw blade for whatever material you happen to be working with – wood, metal or laminate – and away you go.

The best bet is to go for a multi-speed model since this will cut more efficiently all the materials you are likely to be using.

You can probably get by with just two flat-bladed screwdrivers of different sizes for driving slotted screws, plus one cross-point driver for cross-head screws (Pozidriv and Supadriv are the commonest type; a No.2 size screwdriver will drive the most widely used screw sizes).

Although a drill is used to make starter holes for screws, a bradawl is handy to have around especially

9 10 14 15 16 17

25

28 29 30 31

26 27

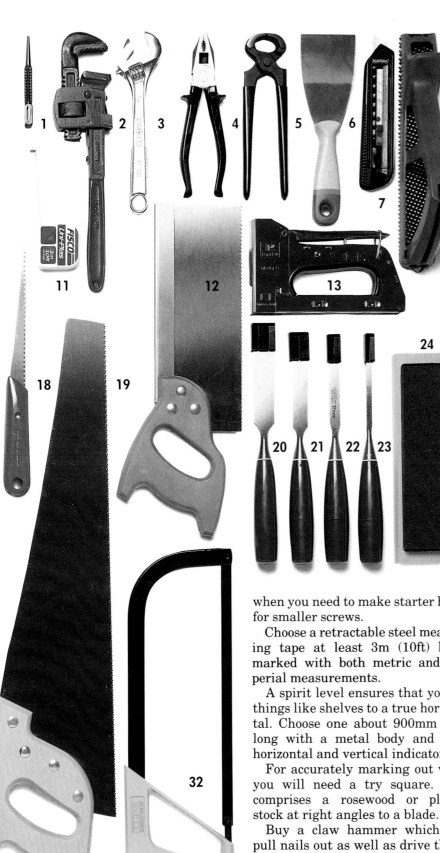

Left: *tools for the jobs.* **1.** *Nail punch* **2.** *Stilson* **3.** *Adjustable spanner* **4.** *Pliers* **5.** *Pincers* **6.** *Filling knife* **7.** *Handyman's knife* **8.** *Surform plane* **9.** *Bradawl* **10.** *Combination try square and spirit level* **11.** *Steel tape measure* **12.** *Tenon saw* **13.** *Staple gun* **14.** *Ratchet slotted screwdriver* **15.** *Fixed-blade Pozidriv screwdriver* **16.** *Ratchet Pozidriv screwdriver* **17.** *Fixed-blade slotted screwdriver* **18.** *Padsaw* **19.** *Panel saw* **20–23.** *Bevel-edged chisels (25mm, 19mm, 12mm, and 6mm)* **24.** *Oilstone and box* **25.** *Extension lead* **26.** *Power jigsaw* **27.** *Electric two-speed hammer drill with chuck key and bits for masonry, metal and wood* **28.** *Spiral ratchet screwdriver* **29.** *Pin hammer* **30.** *Claw hammer* **31.** *Spirit level* **32.** *Hacksaw*

when you need to make starter holes for smaller screws.

Choose a retractable steel measuring tape at least 3m (10ft) long, marked with both metric and imperial measurements.

A spirit level ensures that you fix things like shelves to a true horizontal. Choose one about 900mm (3ft) long with a metal body and both horizontal and vertical indicators.

For accurately marking out wood you will need a try square. This comprises a rosewood or plastic stock at right angles to a blade.

Buy a claw hammer which can pull nails out as well as drive them. In addition, for lighter work, get a pin hammer. A nail punch is useful for when you need to knock a nail

head below the surface of the wood.

Choose a trimming knife with a retractable blade, so you can carry it around safely, and buy a selection of blades for it.

A handsaw (or panel saw) is essential. A good general-purpose one will be about 22in long and have 8 points per inch. A tenon saw will cope with most small sawing jobs on thin boards and on timber up to about 50mm (2in) thick. Choose one with a 300 or 350mm (12 to 14in) blade. Next comes a useful saw called a pad-saw. This will cope with intricate jobs such as cutting out a keyhole. For metal cutting choose a junior hacksaw which takes cheap, throwaway blades, or a full-size model for heavier duty.

Chisels cut joints, recesses for hinges and mortises for locks. You need at least four bevel-edged chisels in 6, 12, 19 and 25mm (¼, ½, ¾ and 1in) widths. Choose plastic handles rather than wooden ones, so you can drive them, if necessary, with your claw hammer instead of a mallet. You will need an oilstone to keep them sharp.

A staple gun is also worth having, since it allows you to make instant fixings of thin sheet materials, fabrics and floorcoverings with one hand free to position the work.

For holding assembled work while the adhesive is setting, some cramps will be invaluable. There are many different patterns on the market nowadays; add them to your tool kit as you find you need them. You will find that you can use your portable workbench as a vice.

For shaping jobs use a Surform. This is a general-purpose plane/rasp, ideal for working with wood and man-made boards; it can tackle metal and plastic too. Surforms come in a range of styles, including flat rasps, planer-files, round files and block planes. All have replaceable blades.

You will often be confronted with nuts and bolts of various types that need tightening or loosening. So an adjustable spanner will come in very handy (you really need two because often you will have to grip a nut as well as a bolt). Choose one small and one medium spanner, to cope with a wide range of nut and bolt sizes.

A nice luxury is a pair of slip-joint pliers. They perform as both pliers and spanner and, having long handles and being adjustable, will grip various shapes and sizes.

Pliers are a real jack-of-all-trades tool – they can grip all sorts of things you may be trying to undo or tighten up, bend things such as stiff wire or metal sheet and crimp wires together if you are doing electrical work. Choose a pair of combination pliers with fine and coarse serrated jaws and a wire-cutter near the pivot

point; plastic handgrips make them more comfortable to use and also provide protection against the risk of shock during electrical jobs. Add a pair of pincers and you will be ready when tacks and nails have to be extracted.

Lots of simple repair jobs around the house involve the use of filler of one type or another. A flexible filling knife with a square-ended blade is invaluable for all these jobs.

A portable workbench is a must. Take it to wherever you are working and it provides a firm, stable surface on which to saw, hammer and drill things to your heart's content. You can also use it as a vice for gripping things as small as a piece of copper pipe or as large as a door.

For successful brickwork you need a bricklaying trowel. To keep your courses level, you can buy a bricklayer's line and pins. Another essential is a pointing trowel for finishing off the pointing between courses neatly. For cutting the bricks and

Above: *a Black & Decker* Workmate *portable workbench.*

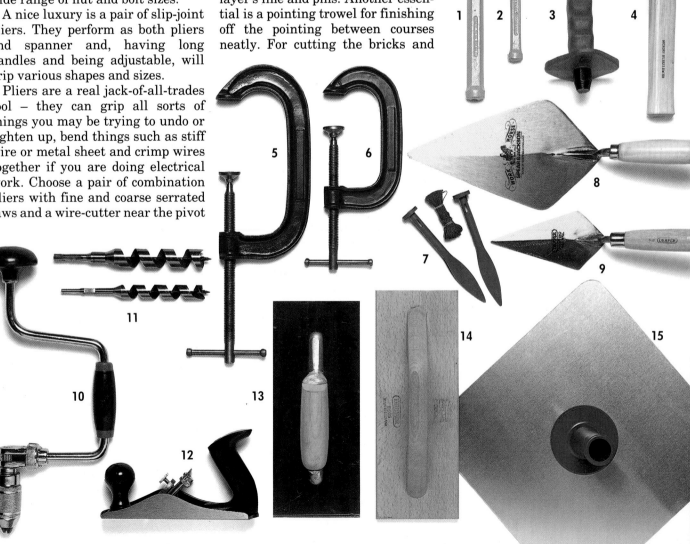

Left: *additional tools.*
1, 2. *Cold chisels*
3. *Bolster chisel*
4. *Club hammer*
5, 6. *G-cramps*
7. *Builder's line and pins*
8. *Bricklayer's trowel*
9. *Pointing trowel*
10. *Ratchet swing brace*
11. *Auger bits*
12. *Smoothing plane*
13. *Steel float*
14. *Wood float*
15. *Hawk*
16. *Circular saw*
17. *Heat gun*
18. *Power planer*
19. *Orbital sander*
20. *Router*

blocks, you need a brick bolster and club hammer. Buy a bolster fitted with a plastic hand shield.

A cold chisel or two will be invaluable for jobs like cutting holes and recesses in walls during plumbing or electrical installations, or for cutting out a damaged brick.

Buy a small cold chisel too; you can use this with your claw hammer for chopping out loose material before making repairs.

Include a shovel for mixing mortar, a wheelbarrow to move it around and a spot board – a sheet of plywood or similar board about 1m square – to place the mortar on alongside your work.

For plastering or rendering work you need another group of specialist tools. First comes the plasterer's trowel or steel float, with which you actually apply the plaster to the wall. To go with it, buy a metal hawk, a square of sheet metal with a handle attached to one side, on which you carry the plaster to the wall surface; you can make one from plywood with a softwood handle if you prefer. A wooden float with nails driven through it is useful as a de-villing tool, to key the wall surface between coats; again, you can improvise one if you wish.

Optional extras include internal and external angle trowels for finishing corners neatly, plus buckets for mixing the plaster and a spot board to hold it.

Additional power tools

A circular saw eliminates elbow work on a host of tough cutting jobs. With the correct disc fitted it can help with everything from cutting up large boards to scoring paving slabs.

For reducing wood to the cross-section you require, you will need either a smoothing plane or an electric power planer.

An orbital sander makes it easy to get a smooth finish on wood or plaster – it is worth getting one with a dust-collecting bag to keep the working atmosphere clear.

Rapidly becoming a favourite is the router. This very versatile machine will make grooves, rebates and ornamental cuts in wood.

Finally, there is the electric heat-gun. You will find this just the job for stripping paint quickly – and helping thaw frozen pipes in winter!

To hire

Although a basic tool kit will enable you to do the vast majority of DIY jobs, every so often you find that a task could be done far more easily, more safely, and to a far better standard if you had specialist tools as might be used by a professional. Some of these tools you will need only once or twice in a lifetime, and the answer is to hire them. Some DIY stores have hire centres, or you can find local hire shops in the Yellow Pages. You will find a vast range of tools: decorating aids such as steam wallpaper strippers; ladders, platforms and trestles, floor cleaning, laying and sanding equipment; saws and sanders; planes and routers; builders' equipment; hammer drills and breakers; plumbing tools; gardening tools and equipment; car maintenance equipment; and miscellaneous items such as floodlights. Here is a selection of useful tools to hire to help you carry out the projects in this book.

Roughcast applicator This applies a Tyrolean finish, or cement roughcast, to exterior walls. Use it to achieve an attractive finish over bricks, blocks or concrete. As you turn the handle, the machine flicks a wet mortar-like mix on to the wall, leaving it with a coarse texture.

Platform tower Ideal for safety when carrying out repairs and decoration at a height. The tower is supplied in sections and you build it up to the height required, fitting a platform of scaffold boards at the height you wish to work. A handrail at the top gives extra safety. When building a tower, check with a spirit level that it is vertical, and adjust the feet to achieve this. For outdoor use, the maximum height for a free-standing tower with a 1.3m (4ft 3in) square base size is 4.5m (14ft 9in) for a static tower, and 3.9m (12ft 10in) for a tower on castors.

Trestles and scaffold board Two trestles with scaffold boards or staging fitted between them to form a walkway make a continuous working platform at a fairly low level – ideal, for example, for indoor ceiling work, or outdoor maintenance on a bungalow.

Industrial vacuum cleaner A powerful industrial-type vacuum cleaner will usually be just the job for cleaning up after work. Most cleaners of this type are suitable for both wet and dry pick-up, so you can use them to clean up wet wallpaper scrapings and water spills as well as wood shavings, sawdust, brick and plaster dust, and even bits of rubble. These machines have powerful suction, and the wide diameter hose does not block easily like that on a domestic vacuum cleaner.

Disc sander/grinder This tool is available in various sizes. Probably a machine with a 115mm (4½in) diameter disc size will be adequate for most jobs – the 178mm (7in) sander/grinder is heavy to manoeuvre for long periods. Use this tool for various metal-grinding jobs, and for rough sanding; it removes material very quickly. Fitted with a suitable cutting disc (there are types for metal and masonry) you can cut and score metal, stone, concrete and brickwork. The smaller machine has a 25mm (1in) maximum depth of cut; the larger machine will cut up to about 50mm (2in) deep.

Concrete mixer The benefits of this machine are considerable. The most easily handled kind is the electric-powered barrow-type tip-up mixer which can be transported by car and handled by one person. To use, add some water first (standing on the right-hand side to avoid being splashed), then add the full amount of cement, then the sand or ballast. As soon as the mix begins to stiffen, add more water. Once it has stopped, never try to restart a loaded mixer as this can burn out the motor. Clean the mixer by running it with water and bits of hardcore.

Light compactor This machine is light in weight, yet it is excellent for compacting bases for concreting and paving. Its vibrating action comes from a petrol engine-driven vibrating plate which creates a centrifugal force equal to 1111kg (2450 lbs). In use, the machine is simply moved backwards and forwards over the area to be firmed. It can also be used to settle blocks into a sand base.

Demolition drill/heavy hammer This tool will break concrete up to 100mm (4in) thick and is ideal for knocking down walls, for example, when two rooms are knocked into one (after the new lintel has been installed). These electric hammers are supplied with removable chisel bits and points.

Post-hole borer A post-hole borer is much more effective than a spade for quickly digging out holes for fence posts and the like. It is a hand-operated tool and by moving the handle back and forth you can quickly cut a hole of about 200mm (8in) diameter.

Tacker gun This hand-held tool is for driving staples into wood and other soft materials. It is very light and quick to use and is ideal for light

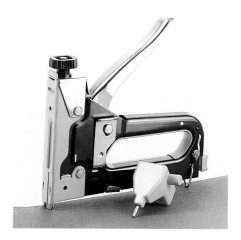

tacking jobs, such as fixing building paper to the underside of rafters for improved loft insulation and draughtproofing. It is also good for upholstery jobs.

Sash cramp Use this tool to hold timbers and timber frameworks together when they are being assembled and glued. It helps you to get tight joints and ensure that the framework is square.

Ceiling prop If you are tackling a job like knocking two rooms into one, you will need several of these to temporarily support the wall above while a new lintel is inserted across the span. They work like giant car jacks and are adjustable from 2 to 3.35m (6 ft 6in to 11ft).

Pressure washer This is a really useful tool for clearing up after building work. It has an electric pump which boosts the pressure of hose water to a powerful water jet that blasts away dirt. It can be used to clean tools and machinery (cars too, on its lowest pressure setting), as well as walls, grimy patios, paths and drives.

Circular saw You may have a small DIY saw, but if there is a lot of woodcutting to do, or large sections to cut up, then it will be well worth hiring an industrial-type circular saw. One with a 228mm (9in) blade will make short work of cutting timber up to 75mm (3in) thick. You can also get special blades for cutting masonry, metals and hard plastics up to 25mm (1in) thick.

Stone splitter A hand-operated hydraulic press which will quickly cut and trim building and paving materials, such as paving blocks, quarry, and concrete tiles, edging

kerbs, interlocking block paving, thermal and breeze blocks, and bricks. It will cut a block of up to 530mm (21in) in length and up to 100mm (4in) thick and is ideal for cutting paving to fit at edges and corners.

Floor sander This electrically-operated drum sander will quickly remove the surface layer of an old timber floor to reveal its original lustre. It has a dust extractor (but you will still need a dust mask), and a complementary hand-operated edging disc sander is available for finishing the edges of the floor and the corners.

Damp-proof injector If you have had trouble with wet or dry rot in a floor, and/or dampness in walls, then one of these machines will allow you to pressure-inject damp-proofing fluid into the masonry or brickwork. You will also need a hammer drill and 10mm (⅜in) masonry bit to make holes in the wall for the injectors.

MATERIALS

Having a good tool kit is only half the battle in DIY. Another vital aspect is choosing the right materials for the job in hand.

A knowledge of materials, their advantages and disadvantages, their suitability for use in certain situations, their durability or lack of it, is essential. You will want to know the amount of maintenance needed to keep them looking good. You need to know about different qualities so that you do not waste any money by buying a better grade than you really need. Conversely, you do not want to buy an inferior grade and find yourself having to do the job again – properly – a short time later.

Another factor to evaluate is your skill. If you are a beginner you will probably prefer a material that is easy to handle and therefore enables you to produce better workmanship.

Finally, and most important, always follow any directions supplied by the manufacturer. Before you start work read and understand them. This section contains useful basic background advice about all the materials used in the projects in the book.

Timber

Nearly all wood used by the do-it-yourselfer is softwood – which is inexpensive and easy to work with. European redwood (sometimes called deal or Scot's pine) is the most readily available, though spruce, Douglas fir and Western red cedar (which is particularly durable exterior grade timber) are all popular.

Softwood is sold in rough and smooth versions. The rough is called *sawn* and is suitable for any work that is to be hidden – a framework for decorative wallboards for example. *Planed* timber is the smooth version which is needed where appearance is important. Planed (or *PAR* – meaning Planed All Round) is slightly thinner than its stated size. If you see 50 × 25mm PAR, you know this means you have to take from 3 to 6mm off both width and thickness to get the actual size.

Before buying timber check that it is sound. Reject any that is warped or has end shakes, cracks or dead knots. Softwood comes in a range of standard metric sizes from 12.5 × 12.5mm (½ × ½in) up to 100mm (4in) thick and 225mm (9in) wide.

Hardwood

Hardwood is much more expensive than softwood and is generally only used for a special decorative effect. Teak, mahogany, iroko and oak are particular favourites. Ramin is a closely textured hardwood with an even grain pattern and is widely used for mouldings.

Timber boards

Timber cladding is often known as *tongue and groove* or *t&g*, since the two edges of each board are specially shaped to give a tongue one side and a groove on the other. The tongue of one piece fits into the groove on the next. These boards are also known as *vee joint* or *matching*.

You will find different designs of tongue and groove, including *open*

Below: *assorted mouldings and timber.*
1. *Half round* **2.** *Square* **3.** *Triangle*
4. *Birdsmouth* **5.** *Quadrant* **6.** *Scotia.*

joint and *close joint,* in both softwood and hardwood. Another type of cladding is called *shiplap,* which is similar, except that the scalloped tongue on one piece fits under a rebate on the next. It is more often used outside as weatherboarding.

Softwood wall cladding is generally 100mm wide. Expect to pay around twice as much for hardwood.

In addition to timber board cladding, you can also get plywood or *MDF (medium-density fibreboard)* faced with wood veneer.

Wall panels

There is a wide selection of wall panels available in 2440 × 1220mm (8 × 4ft) sheets. The more common of these is melamine-faced hardboard or plywood with a woodgrain pattern, which often simulates cladding in oak, pine or cherry.

You can get more elaborate designs, including imitation brick.

Mouldings

There is a wide range of off-the-shelf mouldings available, ready to be glued and pinned into place.

7. Picture rail 8. Dado 9. Moulded skirting 10. Reversible skirting 11. Architrave 12, 13. T&g cladding

Most everyday mouldings are machined either from softwood (usually pine or redwood) or from a cheap hardwood such as ramin.

Architraves are fitted round flush door and window openings to create a decorative and protective border. They are available in styles to match plain and ornate skirtings.

If you are making furniture, whether freestanding or fitted, you may wish or need to use mouldings. There are mouldings for finishing off internal corners and for hiding gaps; the most widely used are *scotia, triangle* and *quadrant* mouldings. For external corners and for some edging jobs, you can choose *right-angle* or *birdsmouth* mouldings.

Then there are several mouldings which are ideal as edgings for man-made boards, where you do not want to see the core material; these include *half-round, twice-rounded, hockey-stick, reeded* and *astragal.* There are also embossed decorative beadings – slim hardwood strips with a three-dimensional design embossed on the top surface. These are the nearest thing to a true

14–17. PAR (planed all around) softwood 18, 19. Sawn softwood 20, 21. Preservative-impregnated sawn softwood.

moulding, and come in a wide range of sizes and patterns.

When you are buying mouldings check that lengths are straight and free from large or dead knots. Watch out for fungal staining, which can be difficult to disguise if you plan a clear finish, and check the grain and colour match between lengths if you are buying large quantities of a particular moulding. Check for surface ripples caused by careless machining, and make sure that edges are sharply cut and undamaged.

Man-made boards

All man-made boards are sold in standard sheets measuring 2440 × 1220mm (8 × 4ft). Smaller panels are sold for convenience.

Standard hardboard has one smooth face and one with a rough mesh pattern. It is weak, so must be supported by a framework and breaks up if it gets wet. However, it is cheap and will easily bend round curves. The commonest thicknesses are 3, 4 and 6mm ($\frac{1}{8}$, $\frac{3}{16}$ and $\frac{1}{4}$in).

Tempered hardboard has been treated to make it water-resistant, and can be used outdoors.

Perforated hardboard is punched with holes (known as *pegboard*), slots or decorative patterns.

12 14 16 18 20

13 15 17 19 21

Medium-density fibreboard (MDF) is far stronger. It will not flake or splinter when cut, and gives a clean, hard edge which does not need disguising like that of other man-made boards. It is available in thicknesses from around 15mm (⅝in) up to 35mm (1⅜in).

Chipboard

Chipboard is a rigid, dense and fairly heavy board. It is strong if reasonably well supported. Screws do not hold well in it. Most grades are not moisture-resistant. Various thicknesses are available but 12, 18 and 25mm (½, ¾, and 1in) are the commonest. Flooring-grade chipboard is denser than other types.

Chipboard is also widely available with the board faces and edges covered with natural wood veneers, pvc or melamine coatings or plastic laminate. These are available in a range of standard shelf sizes – lengths from 610mm (2ft) up to

2440mm (8ft) and widths from 150mm (6in) upwards.

Plywood

The *WBP (weather-and-boil-proof)* grade is suitable for all external uses. *MR (moisture-resistant)* board is used in damp indoor conditions. Use *INT* for internal work in dry conditions only.

Common board thicknesses are 3, 6, 12 and 19mm (⅛, ¼, ½ and ¾in).

Blockboard

Blockboard is a relatively dense, strong board, but it can be hard to get the edges neat if the core end-grain is exposed, and making fixings into this edge can be difficult.

Common thicknesses for blockboard are 12, 18 and 25mm (½, ¾ and 1in). Other sizes are available.

Plasterboards

Plasterboard is available in various sizes and the most common is 12.5mm (½in) thick, 1200mm (4ft) wide and 1800mm (6ft) or 2400mm (8ft) long. A 9.5mm (⅜in) board is also available, but as the 12.5mm board requires less timber framing it is usually more economical.

Gyproc plasterboard has a decorative face with tapered long edges which, when fixed, jointed and treated give a seamless smooth, flat surface ready for decoration.

Duplex plasterboard has a back-

ing of metallised polyester film which is water vapour resistant. When the backing faces a cavity, such as when the board is fixed to timber battens on a wall, it gives improved thermal insulation.

Thermal board combines the qualities of wallboard with the high thermal insulation of expanded polystyrene, to form an insulating lining for walls and ceilings.

Cement, sand and aggregates

Cement, sand and aggregate form the ingredients of concrete, cement rendering and mortar.

Sand can be obtained in various colours from red to brown, also yellow, grey and silver. It may be sharp, that is the grains are angular with sharp edges, or it may be soft with a clay or loam content.

Generally speaking aggregate means large aggregate or gravel.

For most jobs such as garden paths, shed bases, and foundations for garden walls, an all-in aggregate (generally called ballast) is used. This contains all sizes of grit from fine sand up to 20mm gravel.

For all practical purposes cement means ordinary Portland cement, which is grey. White Portland cement, which produces white concrete or mortar, is more expensive.

Dry mixes have a number of advantages for the home user. They are bagged in the right proportions and sold in small quantities which need only the addition of water.

Correct proportioning is important if mortar mixes are to be of the same colour or if concrete is to be of adequate and consistent strength.

The ingredients tend to separate

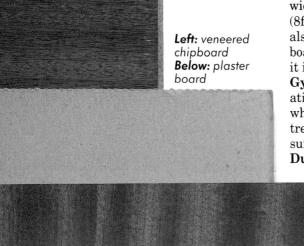

Left: *veneered chipboard*
Below: *plaster board*

Left: *veneered plywood*
Below: *Contiplas*

Left: *teak-faced Contiboard*
Below: *hardboard*

in the bag so, before use, pour the contents on to a clean surface and mix again while dry. Any excess should then be returned to an airtight bag and stored off the ground under shelter or it will go hard.

A standard bag of cement is 50kg, but cement can be found at some DIY stores packed in smaller quantities. Sand and gravel are also packed in 50kg bags.

Plasters

There are basically two groups of plasters. Traditional plasters are applied in two layers; the undercoat (also the backing or browning coat) and the top or finishing coat. Newer types forming the other group are one-coat plasters. By no means have the traditional plasters been superseded by the one-coat plasters; the former are still the most widely used types, but the one-coat plasters generally have slower setting times and are therefore found easier to apply by those who have less experience in plastering.

Browning comes in many versions and the right type is selected according to the surface to which it is to be applied – bricks, blocks, wood lath, one with low water absorption etc. They each have different setting times and can be applied in different thicknesses. It is important therefore to choose the right type and to use it correctly following manufacturer's instructions.

Finishing plasters come in a far smaller range and are selected according to the undercoat used.

Bricks

There are three main types – common; facing; and engineering.

Common bricks are used where appearance does not matter.

Facing bricks have an attractive appearance and are used where the wall will be seen.

Engineering bricks are strong and dense bricks with a uniform colour. They are frost-resistant.

All these types are available in different grades – *internal* quality, *ordinary* quality (for outdoor use in sheltered situations), *special* quality (with good weather resistance).

A standard brick size is 215mm long, by 103mm wide, by 65mm deep ($8\frac{1}{2} \times 4 \times 2\frac{1}{2}$in). The mortar joint will be 10mm ($\frac{1}{2}$in) and this must be added to these dimensions when calculating the number of bricks required.

Building blocks

There are three main types of blocks and many shapes and sizes available to the DIY builder.

Type A blocks – dense aggregate, loadbearing and suitable for most structural uses.

Type B blocks – lightweight loadbearing blocks, easier to handle than type A. Can be used outdoors.

Type C blocks – lightweight, non-loadbearing blocks generally used for internal partition walls.

Various materials are used in the manufacture of blocks including clinker, aerated concrete and pulverised fuel ash. Lightweight blocks may be solid or hollow, and the cavities may be filled with expanded polystyrene foam for additional thermal insulation.

Most blocks are intended to be finished by plastering, rendering, or painting.

Paving slabs

Precast concrete slabs are available in a wide range of sizes. Slabs measuring 460mm (18in) square are the best size to choose – slabs larger than this are very heavy to handle. Slabs may be smooth, textured, or patterned and may be coloured to represent stone, or be made from reconstructed stone.

Crazy paving comprises broken paving slabs which are fitted together in a random pattern.

Concrete paving blocks look like bricks but are much harder and are ideal for driveways. They are laid on a bed of sand and are settled in place using a plate virbrator.

Brick or clay paviours are ideal

Right: pegboard
Below: Laminboard

Right: blockboard
Below: MDF

Right: chipboard
Below: plywood

for paths as they have a natural appearance. They are not as strong as concrete paving blocks. If bricks are used for paving they must be a frost-proof type.

Decorative walling blocks

For screen walls, pierced concrete screen blocks are available in a wide range of designs. Walls of this type need strengthening piers made from matching pilaster blocks.

For decorative garden walls there are various walling blocks made from stone-coloured concrete and reconstructed stone. These are available in single blocks of various sizes and multiple blocks made to represent a section of walling comprising smaller stones.

Brick tiles and stone cladding

These slips are fixed to walls to simulate brick or stone walling. The tiles may be made from fired clay, like real bricks, or aggregate, or plastic material to simulate bricks. The rigid types are available as flat slips, and L-shapes for use at external corners. The plastic types can be heated and bent to form corners. The stone cladding is made from reconstructed stone or plastic to simulate quarried stone. Both types are fixed to the wall using special adhesive. Some are pointed with mortar after fixing.

Ceramic tiles

Ceramic wall tiles are available in many shapes and sizes. They have a gloss or matt glazed finish and may be smooth, embossed or decorated in a wide range of styles. *Universal* tiles or *spacer* tiles have angled edges which automatically give the correct size gap for grouting. *Non-spacer* tiles must have tile spacers fitted between the tiles during laying. Special corner and rounded-over edge tiles are available in some ranges, but the majority of tiles are simply glazed on two or more edges

1. *Wonderplast* 2. *Sirapite plaster* 3. *Thistle plaster* 4. *Mix and point* 5. *Polycell Quick Set cement mix* 6. *Polyplasta* 7. *Polyskim* 8. *Sand cement mortar ready mix* 9. *Sharp sand* 10. *Silver sand* 11. *Soft sand* 12. *Aggregate*

so that they can be used on corners.
Ceramic floor tiles are similar to wall tiles, but they are thicker and stronger to withstand heavy wear.
Quarry tiles are unglazed and can be used on floors indoors and outside (as can some ceramic floor tiles).

Nails

Nails are the easiest and cheapest fixing devices, and if correctly used they are very effective. Use them for joints that will not have to be dismantled.

Round wire plain-head nail – strong, general-purpose nail for use where appearance is of no account. Use a nail three times as long as the thickness of the wood it is holding.
Oval wire brad-head nail – use as round wire nails; the shape of this nail means it is less likely to split the wood than a round nail.
Round wire lost-head nail – use where neatness is important.
Cut clasp or floor brad – these

nails are cut from flat metal sheets and used mainly to fix floorboards.
Clout nails – galvanized for outdoor use (on roofing), and indoors for fixing plasterboard. The galvanized coating prevents rusting.
Annular ring-shanked nails – shanks are ringed for extra grip.
Masonry pin – specially hardened nails for driving into brickwork.
Hardboard pins – copper-plated nails with specially shaped heads for fixing sheets of hardboard.

Screws

Screws are useful for making fixings that may need to be dismantled or adjusted. They can be stronger than nails used without glue, and they are used for attaching metal components, such as hinges, to wood.

The latest screws are threaded for their full length, they have a twin thread that drives twice as fast as a traditional screw, and they have a more parallel shank which is less

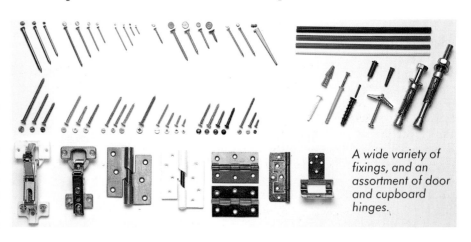

A wide variety of fixings, and an assortment of door and cupboard hinges.

likely to split the wood than the smooth, tapered shank of a traditional screw. Whereas ordinary screws tend to have a single slot head for driving with a flat-blade screwdriver, the latest screws have cross-heads for driving with powered screwdrivers and drill attachments.

Screws are classified by their length (in inches), their diameter by screw gauge number (ie. 6, 8, 10, 12), by material (e.g., steel), by head style (e.g., countersunk, raised or round), and by finish or coating (such as zinc-plated). The best steel screws are zinc-plated to minimise rusting.

Adhesives

A DIY tool kit should contain a selection of adhesives.

PVA is the standard woodworking adhesive for indoor use; for outdoor use choose a *urea-formaldehyde* type (such as Cascamite) which is a powder mixed with water to form a gap-filling paste.

Epoxy-resins (such as Araldite) are two-part adhesives to make strong waterproof bonds between a wide variety of materials. Two-part acrylics (such as Multi-Bond) are similar, but dry clear.

Superglues (cyanoacrylates) are for quick bonding of a wide variety of materials. They are not gap-filling and the parts must fit closely.

Contact adhesives are rubber-based. They are applied to two surfaces which are allowed to dry and which will then bond together on contact. They are useful for bonding large items, such as laminates.

Latex adhesives are rubber-based white liquids which dry clear. They are particularly useful for carpets and fabrics.

Glue guns use adhesive sticks which are melted in the guns and the molten glue is exuded through

Above: *a selection of paving and building materials – paving slabs and paviours, moulded edging stones, bricks, building blocks, and walling blocks.*

the nozzle. They are useful for small repairs on a very wide range of materials.

Fillers

Fillers divide into universal fillers for walls and wood to be finished by painting; plaster fillers; wood fillers for wood to be painted; and natural-coloured wood fillers for wood to have a clear finish.

Universal fillers may be ready-mixed, or be in powder form to be mixed with water. They are simply pressed into place and smoothed down. When dry they can be sanded flat.

Plaster fillers are for walls only. They are cheaper and can be used for quite large-scale repairs.

Two-part epoxy-based fillers are available for wood and metal filling. They are very quick-setting and strong, and are ideal for rebuilding rotted wood as part of wood repair systems. They must be finished by painting.

Foam fillers are for insulating and gap-filling – ideal for use around pipes and gaps between timber frames and walls. They expand as they set.

Plastic wood is wood-coloured and useful for filling small holes and cracks in wood.

Wood stopping is available in a wide range of wood shades.

Mastics and sealants

Used to fill gaps and cracks around the house, mastics and sealants come in various types made for specific purposes; all remain fairly flexible so they are able to cope with degrees of movement.

Decorative sealants are used to fill gaps which are visible; around baths, basins, and shower trays and between ceilings and walls.

Outdoor sealants are used to seal gaps in a building that are prone to reopen. Buy a specialist sealant for the purpose you require.

Paint

Paints divide into three categories – preparatory paints, like primers and undercoats; top-coat paints, such as gloss and emulsion; and special purpose paints, such as masonry and textured paints. Some paints are suitable for both exterior and interior use, others are for either interior use only, or for exterior use only. Check the instructions regarding suitability of use when buying the paint.

DIVIDING A ROOM

Although, at first, dividing a room might seem to be an enormous task for a DIYer there really is not a great amount of skill involved – just some basic hammer and nails carpentry. It is, however, the kind of job that can transform a house, making far greater use of your existing living space.

Everyone will have different ideas as to why they should want to build a partition – perhaps one large room downstairs could be divided into two to provide a separate dining room and lounge. This could also be a way to create a separate lounge so that various members of the family could entertain their own visitors privately without disturbing the rest of the household. Or perhaps someone wants to play records, read quietly or study while everyone else watches the TV . . .

An extra bedroom can solve a lot of problems – especially if you have a growing family or an elderly relative comes to stay. It is also useful to have a spare bedroom for overnight guests or visiting friends and relatives. It need only be of 'box room' proportions yet it can make a world of difference to family lifestyle. Many a family has spent thousands of pounds moving to a new house or extending their existing one to gain an extra bedroom, when for a couple of hundred pounds their problem could have been solved with a simple partition.

There are many other possibilities – a new shower room perhaps, a cloakroom in a large hallway, perhaps an entrance lobby to conceal the living room from the front door. Step back and take an objective look at your own house and think how a partition could improve it.

The standard way of making a partition is to build a framework of timber and then line it on both sides with plasterboard. This is known as a stud partition wall and it is the method used to build nearly all the internal walls of modern houses.

There are certain requirements that must be adhered to when a new room is created. For example, if you are making a bedroom you may need to create an extra window which will have to be about one-twentieth of the floor area of the room. If you want to make a downstairs loo you cannot have it leading directly off a kitchen; the regulations state that there must be two doors with a small lobby between the rooms. The safest bet is to have a chat with the local planning department at the town hall or to employ an architect to advise you. Professional instruction can often save a great deal of money or even reveal better ways of tackling a project.

A lot of thought at the planning stage will make life much easier when installing a partition wall. It can also make all the difference later on if you need to get at the household services.

First, where will the wall be positioned in relation to the floor joists below and the ceiling joists above?

The best bet is to run it either at right angles to the floor joists (parallel with the floorboards) or, if parallel to the floor joists, sited on one. If neither is possible, plan to insert extra timbers between the joists to support the wall. These timbers should be fixed at 600mm (24in) centres.

A point to bear in mind is that the new wall will make it difficult to lift floorboards which it covers (especially if the wall is parallel with the joists); if access is required through these to reach electrical or plumbing fittings, it will make things more convenient if you cut any relevant floorboard short of the intended wall position so that it can be lifted in the future.

As far as the ceiling is concerned, it will again be easiest if the wall runs at right angles to the joists (which may not run the same way as the floor joists) or, if parallel, coincides with a joist so that the head plate can be screwed into the joist. Never rely simply on screwing to the ceiling itself. If the new wall is to be parallel with, but between the joists, add supporting timbers.

Side support is important too. With solid walls, screws and wall plugs can be used. Hollow partition walls will be more difficult – it is best to position the new wall so that it coincides with a vertical stud in the existing partition wall.

You will also want to think about putting electric wiring within the wall itself, for socket outlets and light switches. There is no problem in running cables inside a stud partition wall, except when you come to a horizontal nogging (including the head and sole plate). You will have to drill the holes in these to take any necessary cables.

When it comes to fitting socket outlets or light switches, there are two ways of going about it. You can insert a timber support when the framework is being built, or use special plasterboard mounting boxes. Special timber supports are usually better and can also be made so that they provide extra support for the plasterboard where it is cut away (with a padsaw or jigsaw) to fit the switch or socket outlet. Extra timbers will, of course, be needed for doorways or windows.

Finally, you will need to think about cupboards, basins and other heavy fixings which may be hung on the wall, for which you will want extra noggings. Shelves are not usually a problem as you can screw the shelf brackets or uprights for adjustable shelving directly into the vertical studs. However, it is most unlikely that heavy cupboards and basins will have their fixing holes at exactly the correct distance apart.

A horizontal nogging on which to hang a radiator might be needed. If you are running the pipes for this (or for anything else) inside the partition, do not use fittings inside the wall where they will be inaccessible.

The final consideration with a partition wall is what you are going to do where it meets the existing wall.

Other features to consider are the skirting and any coving or picture rails there may be. A problem may arise if you want to match the existing fittings so that they continue on to the new wall. With an older house you may not be able to find exactly matching mouldings, though it is possible to have them made, or to cut your own with a router. It may be, however, that you will have to take out the existing skirtings and insert new ones all around the room. This is a very simple carpentry job.

The Framework

The main framework is constructed from 75 × 50mm (3 × 2in) sawn timber, fixed so that the 75mm side forms the thickness of the wall before the plasterboard is applied.

The top member (called the head plate) and a bottom member (called the sole plate) are joined by vertical timbers known as studs. Fix studs 600mm (24in) apart (centre to centre). Sheets of plasterboard 1.2 × 2.4m (4 × 8 ft) can be placed across three studs with their edges supported.

Horizontal members – called noggings – provide extra strength as well as fixing points for heavy wall fixtures (such as kitchen cabinets).

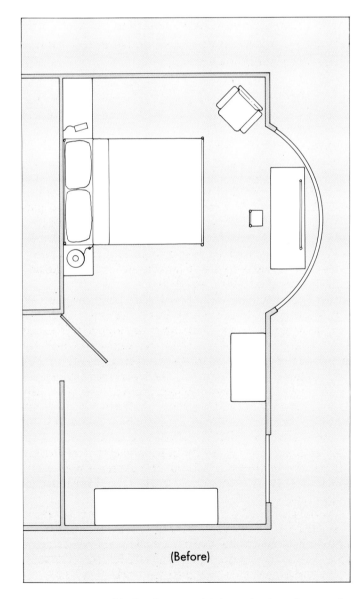

A room very suitable for division: this large bedrom has much underutilized space.

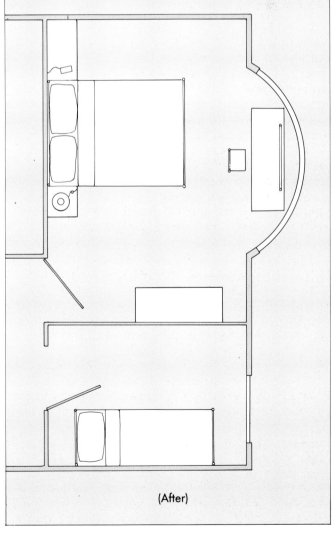

Simple dividing walls have created a useful single bedroom from the larger room.

Extra members may also be needed around other fittings such as doors or light switches.

The framework is nailed together with 100mm (4in) wire nails.

The head plate of the frame is screwed to the ceiling joists; the sole plate is nailed to the floor joists and, if necessary, the end studs are screwed to the side walls.

In a solid floor the sole plate is secured by wall anchors fixed in holes drilled in the floor. A bituminous damp-proof membrane is needed below the sole plate.

Insulation

A plasterboard partition built from 12.7mm (½in) thick boards is suitable for dividing a relatively quiet room such as a bedroom – normal conversation can be heard but not clearly enough to be understood. If you need to achieve better sound insulation than this, use two layers of 12.5mm (½in) thick plasterboard on each side of the 75 × 50mm (3 × 2in) frame, cutting the sheets so the joints between them are staggered. You should then find that even a loud conversation can only just be heard on the other side of the partition but cannot be distinguished. The thermal insulation between the timber stud uprights does offer a slight improvement in sound insulation but its main function is to keep heat in the main room, thereby saving fuel by preventing heat permeating into a spare room which may not be frequently used.

In a loft, a vapour barrier should be included under the plasterboard.

Building the framework

Mark the exact position of the wall on the floor and ceiling and use a small piece of 75 × 50mm (3 × 2in) timber on the ceiling to mark the position of the head plate. Then use a plumb line to align the sole plate. Mark its exact position on the floor.

Cut the sole plate to length and nail it every 600mm (24in), into the joists or extra timbers below. In a solid floor use wall anchors. Cut the head plate to fit, and drill holes in it

1 Snap a string chalk line along the ceiling as a guide for fixing the head plate.

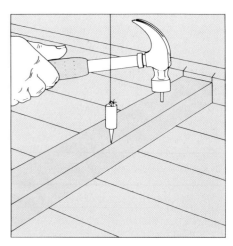

2 Nail the sole plate to the floor, or use screws if you are fixing it to a solid floor.

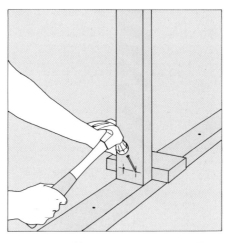

6 Use an offcut to support a stud so that it does not slip while it is nailed to the sole plate.

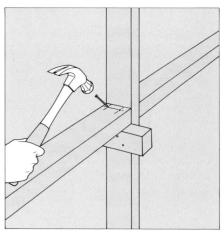

7 Noggings can meet each other exactly or be slightly offset. Support it with an offcut while nailing.

to take the securing screws. Offer up the head plate in place and drill pilot holes in the joists above. Secure the head plate with 100mm (4in) gauge no 10 screws. Check with a plumb line that the two plates are in the right position before driving the nails and screws home. Precise alignment is vital.

Mark out the positions of the doorway and then the studs at 600mm (24in) centres.

Cut the vertical studs to fit between the head and sole plate. Do not cut all the studs in one go; measure and cut each one separately – the floor and ceiling may not be parallel. Each stud should be a push

fit between the two plates. Make cutouts in the end studs to fit around skirtings if necessary.

The end studs are fitted first and these should be positioned vertically, using packing pieces between the stud and wall if necessary. To secure the end studs, use a frame fixing with screw nails. With this, a hole can be drilled right through the stud and into the wall, and the plug pushed home.

If you are fixing the new wall to an existing stud partition, screw into a stud on this.

Now you can nail the studs in position. With skew nailing, the stud will tend to be forced sideways

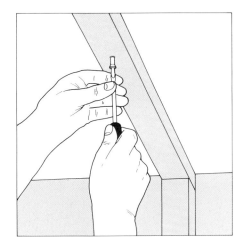

3 Use long screws to fix the head plate firmly into the ceiling joists above the plaster.

4 Cut vertical studs very carefully to length so that they are a tight fit when in place.

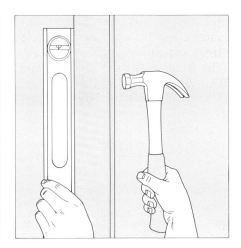

5 Tap each stud into place and check with a spirit level to make sure that it is vertical.

8 If a door frame is required, the top should be cut into the studs so that it is firmly supported.

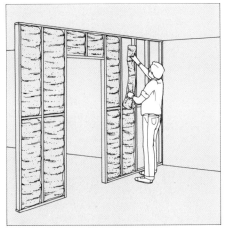

9 Use glassfibre for sound and thermal insulation, especially between a bathroom and bedroom.

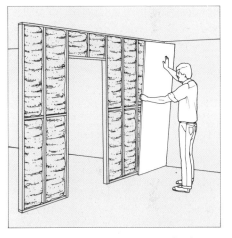

10 Then nail the sheets of plasterboard carefully in place to complete the wall.

as you drive in the first nail, so nail an offcut on to the sole plate against the side of the stud before you start. Drive in two 100mm (4in) nails from the other side, remove the offcut, and put one in from the side where the offcut was. Do this again for the head plate, checking that each stud is vertical. Mark the position of the studs on both floor and ceiling. This will serve as a guide when fixing the plasterboard. You can make skew nailing easier by drilling holes for the nails first.

The horizontal noggings which brace the studs can now be fitted about halfway up. If they are slightly staggered, you can drive the nails in from the side of the stud into the end of the nogging. Work out exactly where you want to position any extra noggings for heavy cupboards. Mark the position of the noggings on the studs.

The size of the doorway should be the size of the door, plus 4mm (⅛in) for clearance, plus the thickness of the door casing – this will be just less than 50mm (2in). Fit the vertical studs on either side of the door, cut through the sole plate and remove the section across the doorway.

In some situations it will be desirable to include a window in the wall – for example, where a lobby has been built around the front door. If the door is glazed to admit light to the main living room this will now be shut out by the lobby walls, so, including a window in the partition may be important.

To make a 'window' in a stud partition wall position 4mm (¼in) glass between pieces of 50mm (2in) moulding, planed down if necessary to fit. A thin bead of putty will stop the glass from rattling.

Fixing the plasterboard

Full details of how to fix and finish plasterboard are given on pages 36–8. Here it is important to note a couple of points on fixing the boards to the frame.

1 Cut away the soleplate from within the door frame, keeping the blade flat against the studs.

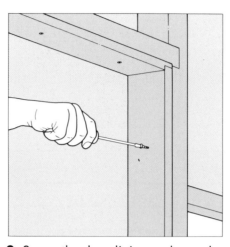

2 Screw the door lining to the studs. Note that the sides are let into the top with housing joints.

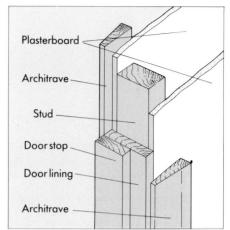

3 Pin the door stops to the lining. Correct positioning is important to allow the door to close.

Plasterboard
Architrave
Stud
Door stop
Door lining
Architrave

4 To fix the architrave, first cut both uprights to length, mitred at the top, and nail them lightly to the frame.

5 Place the top piece upside down on the uprights and mark the position of the cutting line.

6 Mitre both ends of the top piece and check for fit. Nail it to the top frame and nail through the mitres.

Fixing

Cut the boards slightly under length. It takes two people to hold them (ivory side out) against the frame. Butt the paper-covered long side edges tightly together and nail into the timbers at around 150mm (6in) centres, using galvanized plasterboard nails. Keep the nails at least 13mm (½in) away from the edges of the boards and drive them in so the large round heads just dent the surface without breaking the paper lining.

Fix the plasterboards on one side of the frame, stuff the glass fibre insulation blanket (same as loft insulation roll) in position, then fix the plasterboards on the other side of the frame.

The door frame

With the main framework completed and the vertical timbers forming the doorway fixed in place and accurately aligned, the remainder of the door frame is now ready for building and facing with architraves.

Cut off the part of the timber sole plate that is lying across the doorway, flush with the vertical timbers. Keep the side of the saw tight up against the vertical timber to get a neat cut.

At the top of the frame fix a nogging. Let the ends of the nogging into the vertical uprights by about 12mm (½in). Use a tenon saw to cut out the sides of the slot then use a bevel-edged chisel to remove the waste. Work inwards from both sides of the slot. When the nogging is sitting tightly in place, fix it by skew nailing into the uprights.

Next fix the door linings. They must be wide enough to cover the framework and the plasterboard on either side of the wall. Bearing in mind that the timber framework is 75mm thick (actual size, since sawn softwood is used) and that the plasterboard on either side is 12.5mm thick, you should use 100 × 25mm

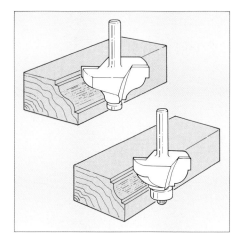

7 You can use cutter heads with a router to shape new skirtings if you are unable to buy matching moulding.

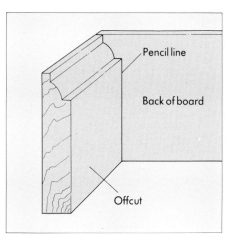

8 To join skirtings neatly first turn the board around and mark its profile on the back.

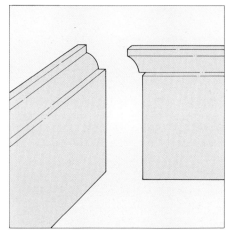

9 Using a padsaw and tenon saw carefully cut out the shape so that it fits over the adjoining length.

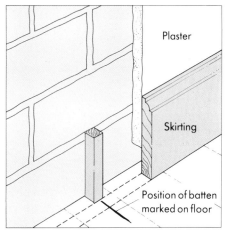

10 Wood blocks set in the wall are for fixing the skirtings. Mark their position on the floor.

the lining. Mark a line all around the lining so that all three parts of the stop will be accurately positioned.

The final job is to fit architrave all around the frame (to conceal the joint between the lining and the plasterboard) and new skirtings. The biggest problem here could be in finding architrave with the correct profile. This is not likely to be a problem in a modern (say 20-year-old or newer) house. However, in older houses, both architraves and skirtings are likely to be far more ornate in profile. If you need to match up then you might have to have them specially cut (which could be expensive) or you could possibly form your own using a router and appropriate cutter heads. Another possibility is to build up the required shape using a mixture of moulding shapes pinned and glued to each other.

The last option would be to replace all architraves around other doors in the room and the skirtings.

It is important to mitre the architrave neatly at the top corners where the horizontal section meets the two verticals. Fix it using 38mm (1½in) lost-head nails driven below the surface. Use pins to secure the mitre joints at the top edges. You can fix the skirtings similarly by nailing through into the vertical studs. It is a good idea to mark the position of the studs on the floor before fixing plasterboard, so that they can be found easily.

Should you decide to replace existing skirting boards in an old house, prise them carefully away from the wall. They will probably be fixed in the traditional way – nailed into wooden blocks set into the brickwork. Refit replacement skirtings by nailing them to the same blocks (so, again, mark their positions on the floor). You can, however, fix narrow modern skirtings using screws or even panel adhesive. Where skirtings join at corners, use an offcut to scribe the required profile onto one of the boards so that you can cut it neatly to fit.

(4 ×1in) planed softwood for the linings. You may need to plane down the softwood to get an exact fit.

Although a simple butt joint can be used to fix the two uprights of the lining to the horizontal member, it is better to cut a housing joint. Screw the lining to the framework timber. Use No.8 countersunk screws so that the screw heads can be left below the surface and the holes filled in to conceal them.

Next, fit a door stop to the lining. This can be simple, square-edge planed softwood or a moulding. In either case, 50 × 12.5mm (2 × ½in) is a reasonable size for a 100 × 25mm lining. Mitre the door stop at

the top corners and fix it to the lining using pins and glue. Use a nail punch to sink the pin heads below the surface and, again, fill the holes to conceal the heads. The positioning of the stop is important since it must allow the door to close neatly against it. If you set it too far forward, the door will not close; too far back and the door will rattle around in draughts, since it is unsupported. To find the correct position, measure the thickness of the door and then transfer this dimension to the door lining. So if, for example, you are using a 37mm (1½in) door you should set the face of the door stop 37mm back from the front edge of

DOORS

After painting and decorating, replacing doors is probably the next most effective way to smarten up your home.

The front door is the main entrance to your house. It should do a lot more than just look handsome – it should be secure enough to keep out opportunist and determined burglars, it should keep out a howling gale and make certain that expensive heat stays inside, and it should keep out driving rain. It is important to choose a door which is in keeping with the style of your house – otherwise you could be creating the opposite effect to what you intend.

Internal doors can also contribute substantially to the decor and appearance of your home and add to its overall attractiveness and its market value.

Fundamentally, there are two types of door – flush doors and traditional panel doors. Both are available in many styles, finishes and sizes.

Flush doors consist of a cellular core, sandwiched between two panels, with solid timber rails, stiles and lock block. The components are bonded together with resin adhesives to give a lightweight but very strong door. The panels are usually flat, but they can be shaped to give the effect of a panelled door.

Some flush doors have an opening to take a panel of glass. There are also fire-check flush doors in which the core of the door is a fire-resistant material which gives 30 minutes or a full one-hour fire resistance. Such doors are required by law to give access to an integral garage, and where a house has been converted into flats, but for your own peace of mind, it is also sensible to fit a fire door to the kitchen where it is most likely that a house fire could start.

Another type of flush door is the high-security door which is a door and frame designed to withstand even sledgehammer blows. All types of flush doors are available in exterior and interior qualities.

Facings can be suitable for painting, or be fully finished veneers. A very wide selection of veneers is available to suit every taste; among the most popular veneers today are teak, rosewood, afrormosia, sapele and oak. They can be supplied fully finished or unfinished for sanding and lacquering.

Panelled doors went out of fashion in favour of the flush door, but now they are regaining popularity, especially in the form of hardwood exterior doors and as glass-panelled doors. The rails and stiles are mortised and tenoned and a wide rail is provided for the letter plate. Hardwood doors may have four or more raised and fielded (sunken border) panels, while softwood doors, which are intended for painting, normally have panels of exterior grade plywood. Both types of doors can be partially or fully glazed.

HANGING A DOOR

Saw off the horns or remove the protective plywood that covers the ends of the stiles to prevent them from splitting in transit. Next try the door in the opening with a helper holding it in place on the outside, if necessary using wedges to support it at the correct height. With a pencil held against the frame, mark around the edge of the frame so that when the door is in position there will be a 2mm ($^1/_{16}$inch) gap all around the edges. Saw across the bottom of the door and plane the edges until the door fits in the opening. Take a couple of extra shavings off the leading edge of the door as well, so it will not strike the frame as it closes.

Cut internal doors square across the bottom so that they will just clear the floor covering, although rising butt hinges can be fitted if the floorcovering is fairly thick on the opening side of the door.

External door frames often have a water bar at the bottom and to prevent draughts the door should close up against this. This usually means that a rebate or step must be cut in the bottom of the door. It is best to cut this rebate with a circular power saw and clear up the waste with a sharp chisel.

If a new door is being fitted in an old frame, the door should be wedged in the opening so that the hinge positions can be marked on the edge of the door. Just fit one screw in each hinge while trying the fit of the door and adjust the depth of the hinge recesses if necessary.

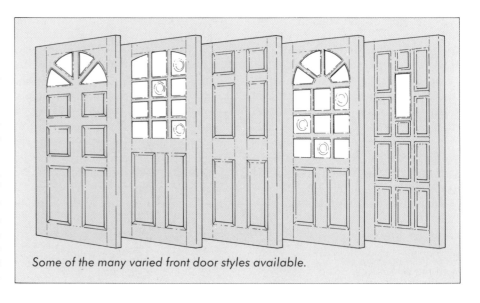

Some of the many varied front door styles available.

1 Get someone to hold the door in position then mark off in pencil where it has to be trimmed.

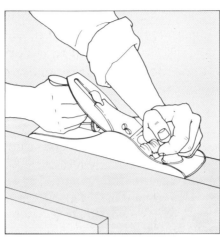

2 Use a plane to trim off excess wood. Check the door in the frame before fitting hinges.

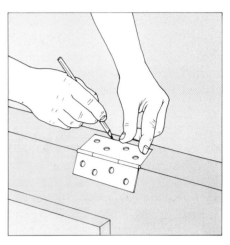

3 Hanging the door starts with marking the position of the hinges. Three 100mm (4in) butts are needed.

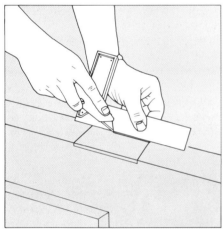

4 Use a knife to cut-in the outline of the hinges before starting to chisel the recess.

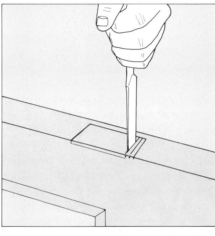

5 Cut out the hinge recess by chopping across the wood grain at close intervals using a wide chisel.

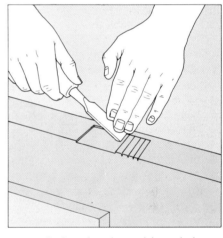

6 With the chisel used bevel down, remove the short pieces of wood and level the slot base.

7 Drill pilot holes for the screws before they are driven home, flush with the hinge flap.

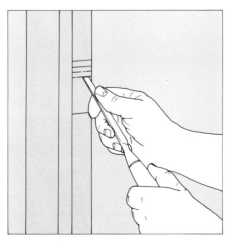

8 Support the door in the frame while you mark the hinge positions. Then cut the recesses.

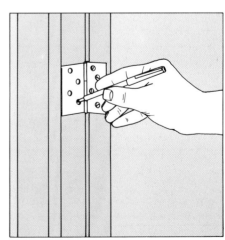

9 Mark the positions of the screws and drill pilot holes. Then try the door with one screw in each hinge.

SECURITY

The most important aspect of a front door is that it offers complete security. Remember, however, that the strongest door in the world, fitted with the best security devices available, can only be as strong as its frame. So check first that this is solid and well anchored.

On a front door you should have two deadlocking locks – 'mortise' and 'rim'. The mortise lock doubles the security; the rim lock is an up-market version of the familiar but insecure cylinder nightlatch.

A mortise lock is fitted into a large slot cut into the door so it fits flush with the door. (You need a brace and bit – or a flat bit – and a chisel plus a pad saw for the keyhole.)

Rim locks are fitted with one part on the inside surface of the door and the other part in a hole cut through the door. Rim locks are easier to fit, but are more obtrusive.

A security bolt is an extremely effective deterrent against forced entry and is very simple to fit. Two bolts should be fitted to each of the back and side doors of your house – one just above the bottom rail and the other just below the top rail. These are in addition to, and not in place of, a good quality five-lever security mortise lock.

Security bolts can also be used to fasten interior doors which have not

got locks, but there is some controversy over whether interior doors should be locked or not. A compromise seems to have been reached that the interior doors should be locked at night when you are in bed, so that an intruder would be confined to the room where he has entered the house; he would be reluctant to force a door open since this would create a noise. Leave them unlocked when you are out during the day as the intruder will do extra damage forcing the doors open and be less concerned about making a noise.

Hinge bolts

The hinge side of the door is often overlooked. While there is an arsenal of devices protecting the lock side, many a burglar will simply kick in the hinge side. Hinge bolts are very simple to fit; the bolt is screwed to the edge of the door and a recess is drilled in the frame. When the door is closed the bolt slots into the recess. Fit two bolts, one at the top and one at the bottom of the door. Hinge bolts are especially advisable on exterior doors which open outwards.

A security chain is desirable since it allows the front door to be opened sufficiently to check the identity of visitors before they are able to gain admittance. This sort of device is essential for the elderly or anyone

living alone. There are all sorts of chains from simple ones to those which incorporate an alarm which will sound if the chain is forced.

A door viewer is another useful asset. These fit into the door at eye level and give the houseowner a wide-angled view of the doorstep.

Furniture

Although this is not just for decoration, functional items such as letterboxes and knockers can be highly ornate. There is a tremendous choice.

Your house number should be clearly displayed on the door if it is not visible somewhere else. The letterbox may be either horizontal or vertical depending on the available space, the shape and the type of front door. You could fit a decorative brass escutcheon plate for the mortise lock keyhole – there is no harm in advertising that you have a decent lock. It is also a good idea to have a knob fitted on the outside of the door.

GLAZED DOORS

Whether insulation, aesthetic appeal or security is your priority the proper selection of glass can make a world of difference. External and internal doors can be glazed in many different ways.

FITTING A CYLINDER RIMLATCH

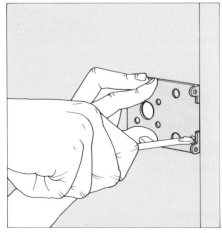

1 Drill a hole through the door for the cylinder; fix lock mounting plate.

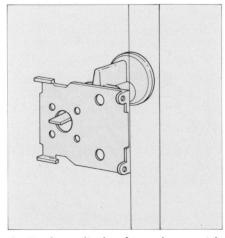

2 Fit the cylinder from the outside and cut the connecting bar to length.

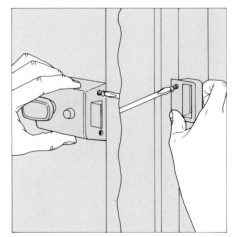

3 Secure the lock to the baseplate and screw the lock to the frame.

FITTING A LETTERPLATE

1 Use a brace and bit to drill holes for the fixing bolts.

2 Drill holes then chisel out the opening, working from both sides.

FITTING A HINGE BOLT

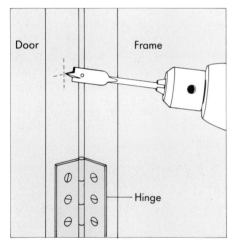

Door Frame

Hinge

1 Make a hole in the door edge and tap in the bolt.

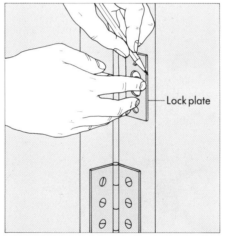

Lock plate

2 Drill a mating hole in the frame and screw on the locking plate.

FITTING A RACK BOLT

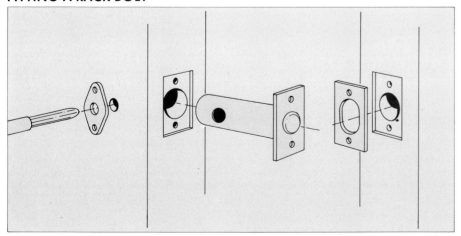

1 The lock is fitted into the edge of the door. A keyhole is drilled, from one side only. A mating hole for the bolt is then drilled into the frame.

Patterned glass is available in a wide variety of designs. Different levels of translucency are possible. A pattern that lets in light, but cannot be seen through, may be all right for the front door, whereas a minimal pattern that allows clear vision may be needed for the back.

Solar control glass can be tinted or coated to any required degree to reduce glare and keep rooms cooler and furnishings unfaded. Up to four-fifths of sunlight can be excluded.

Toughened glass is up to five times stronger than ordinary glass. If it breaks, it shatters into little pieces. It cannot be cut or processed, so it is essential to order the right size.

Laminated glass is particularly recommended where there is a security risk. It consists of two or more panes of ordinary glass, with a special clear plastic membrane in between so that even if the glass shatters, the pieces adhere harmlessly to the plastic and still give protection. This glass can be made very strong and can be tinted for solar control.

Wired glass consists of welded wire mesh inserted between two sheets of glass during the manufacturing process. The wire holds the glass together in the event of cracking. Wired glass is very resistant to flames and smoke and when made to appropriate B.S. standards has a one hour fire rating. It can be clear, rough cast for privacy or patterned for beauty and is strongly advised for doors leading from a house directly to a garage or any situation where fire could be a hazard.

Choosing glass

You must first choose the right thickness. For 4mm (⅛in) glass, for instance, there is a maximum recommended area of about ½ sq m (5 sq ft) whereas for 6mm (¼in) it is 2.4 sq m (26 sq ft) For 6mm (¼in) toughened or laminated glass, however, there is a maximum area of 4 sq m (43 sq ft) for toughened and 3 sq m (32 sq ft) for laminated.

BLOCKING A DOORWAY

When you are planning alterations to the layout of a room, it is quite common to find that the existing doorway gets in the way of the improvements you would like to carry out. For example, it could interrupt a run of kitchen units. In a lounge it could perhaps stop you from placing an item of furniture such as a sofa in the place where you really want it. The answer in cases like these could be to fit a new doorway and block up the old one. When you knock two rooms into one, this again could leave you with a redundant doorway.

In most cases you will want to block up the opening so that when the job is finished there will be no trace of the original doorway. This will involve building a block or timber stud wall which is then plastered over without leaving a visible patch. The two ways of doing this are shown here and over the page.

An alternative is to make a feature of the doorway with recessed shelves, while the back of the shelves can be filled with two layers of plasterboard to leave a smooth wall on the other side of the old doorway.

If you choose to make shelves, remove the old frame and line the opening with 25mm (1in) thick planed timber to the width of the wall. Cut housings (slots) in the timber uprights on each side of the opening to support the shelves. On one side of the opening nail up plasterboard, and on the other side nail a decorative architrave moulding.

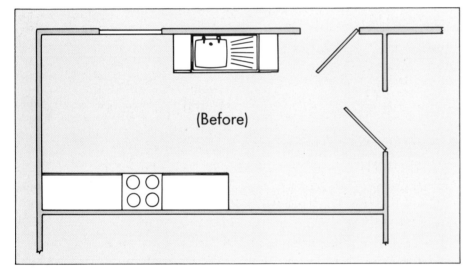

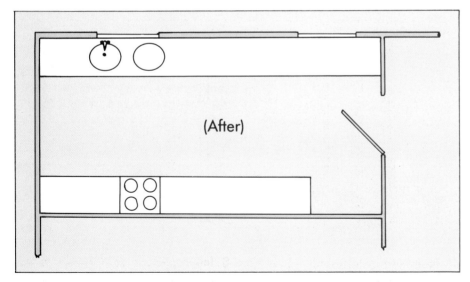

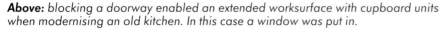

Above: blocking a doorway enabled an extended worksurface with cupboard units when modernising an old kitchen. In this case a window was put in.

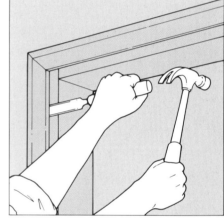

1 After removing the door prise off the architrave with a chisel.

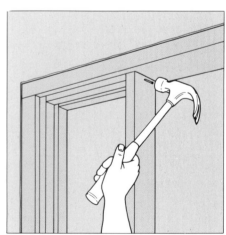

5 If the opening is more than 600mm (24in) wide, nail a central stud to support the plasterboard.

BLOCKING A DOORWAY WITH A TIMBER STUD PARTITION

It is very simple to block a doorway with a timber stud partition frame, but it is necessary to ensure that the edges of the new plaster are reinforced with tape to prevent the differential expansion between the timber framing and the bricks or blocks in the wall from causing a network of cracks around the edges of the alteration.

Remember also when you are deciding what materials to use that a stud wall does not have the same soundproofing qualities as a plastered solid brick or block wall.

Preparing the opening

Start by removing the door and then use an old chisel (it does not have to be sharp) to lever off the decorative architrave from around the opening. Also prise off the door stop from around the doorframe lining.

Measure across the door opening at floor level and cut a timber sole plate to this size from 50mm (2in) thick timber which is as wide as the door frame. Nail this to the floor in the door opening.

Using 25 × 38mm (1 × 1½in) timber, cut two battens to fit in each side of the opening. Nail the battens in place to form a 12.5mm (½in) deep rebate which will allow 12.5mm thick plasterboard to be nailed in place with its surface flush with the framework.

If the opening exceeds 600mm (24in) wide a vertical timber should be nailed in place as a central fixing point for the plasterboard. This timber should be 12.5mm (½in) less in width than the frame lining and can be fixed in place, also recessed 12.5mm (½in), by skew (angle) nailing at top and bottom of the opening.

Twin battens spaced and sized in the same way should then be fixed to the sole plate and at the head of the

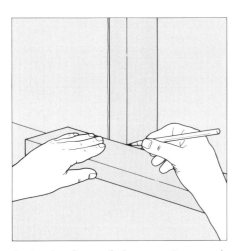

2 At the foot of the opening mark off the timber sole plate to size and nail it in place.

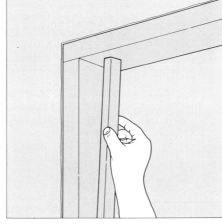

3 For each side of the opening cut two full-length battens to the height of the opening.

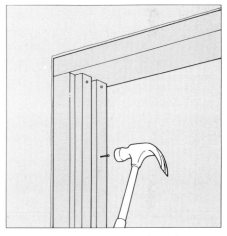

4 Nail the battens so that they are set back 12.5mm (½in) from the front edge to accept the plasterboard.

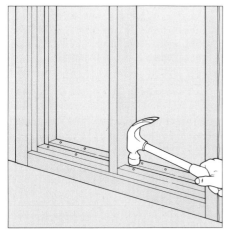

6 Then fix twin battens to the sole plate and head of the frame at each side of the upright.

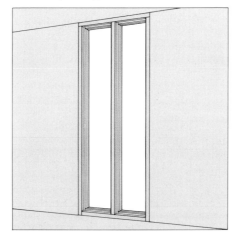

7 Nail the plasterboard in place at each side of the opening using plasterboard nails.

8 Insert plasterboard nails into the supporting timbers 150mm apart. Finish as required.

frame to complete the framing for the plasterboard partition.

Fixing the plasterboard

Cut the plasterboard to the size of the opening. If, after fixing, it will lie flush with the surface of the surrounding walls it can be fixed cream side outwards ready for direct decoration. However, if it is below the level of the surrounding walls, fix it grey side outwards so that it can be finished with a skim coat of plaster to bring the surface level with the surrounding wall surface.

Nail the plasterboard in place with galvanized plasterboard nails inserted into the timber framework at 150mm (6in) intervals.

If the board has been fixed ready for direct decoration, remove surrounding wallpaper and apply a PVA bonding agent to the exposed timber frame. Fill around the edges of the board with a sandable wall filler and while this is still wet press plasterboard joint tape into the surface. Allow this to set, then apply another layer of joint filler, which you should feather out on the surrounding wall to ensure a flat surface.

If the board has been fixed ready for a skim coat of board finish plaster, apply joint filler around the edges of the board and while this is still wet press joint reinforcing tape into the surface. When this has dried, skim over the surface with finish plaster, dragging a flat piece of timber across the opening while the plaster is wet to get a flat surface. Finally polish the surface of the plaster as it dries using a steel plasterer's float dampened.

BLOCKING A DOORWAY WITH BRICKS OR BLOCKS

There are two advantages in using bricks or blocks to block up an opening. First, they have excellent acoustic properties, and secondly, because the materials are the same as those

1 If the new wall is to be bonded by chopping out recesses in the adjacent walls, do this first.

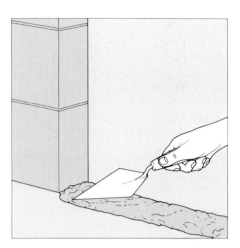

2 On a solid floor, lay a bed of mortar ready for the first course of blocks.

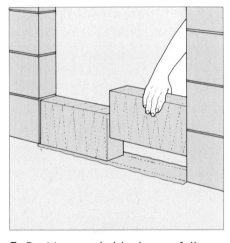

5 Position each block carefully so that it is aligned with its neighbour at top, bottom and sides.

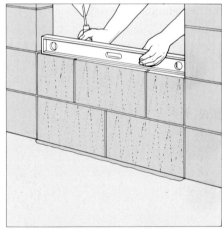

6 Tap each block down with the trowel handle so it is firmly bedded and check that it is level.

used in the construction of the wall, surface cracks around the alteration are very unlikely to open up later.

Preparing the opening

Start by removing the existing woodwork from the old door opening. Saw through the doorframe jambs at each side using an old saw. Prise the jambs away from the wall using a sturdy lever, such as a wrecking bar. Remove the lower section first, then lever away the upper part of the jamb from the head of frame. Finally, lever down the head of the frame. Probably the old frame will be spiked into the wall with large nails: if any of these are left in the

wall once the timber frame has been pulled away, extract them or cut them off flush with the walling bricks or blocks.

The next step is to cut back the plaster by about 150mm (6in) on each side of the opening. This will reveal the bricks or blocks of the wall and help you decide whether it is best to use bricks or blocks to fill in the opening. Use whichever is the most convenient to maintain the bond of the wall.

It is important that the new brickwork or blockwork is keyed into the wall on each side to ensure that cracks do not open up later around the join. There are various ways to

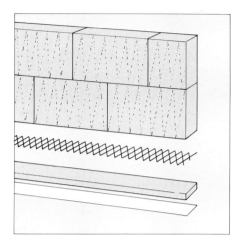

3 On a timber floor, nail a timber sole plate over a strip of DPC and lay the blocks on reinforcing mesh.

4 'Butter' one end of each block before laying it on a bed of mortar. Final thickness should be 10mm.

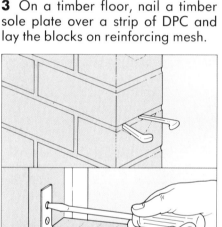

7 With blocks it is possible to get a good key into adjoining walls by using wall ties or nails.

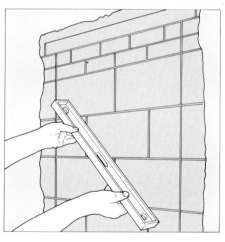

8 Keep checking that the wall is level and vertical. Use bricks to fill in the gap at the top of the opening.

key-in the new wall. An easy method is to use galvanized metal ties. Screw these to the side walls so that the protruding ends of the ties will be buried in the new brickwork or blockwork mortar joints. An alternative is simply to drive large-cut clasp nails into the mortar joints of the surrounding brickwork so that the protruding heads will be bedded in the mortar joints of the new wall. Drive the nails at an angle so they are splayed out to form a strong bond.

For a really strong bond you can tie the new wall to the adjacent walls by chopping recesses in alternate courses. With a brick wall this means chopping out a half-brick at about every fourth course. With a block wall, chop out quarter blocks in alternate courses. Use a club hammer and bolster chisel for this.

Building the wall

Use ready-mixed brick or block-laying mortar or mix your own from one part cement to six parts soft sand. On a solid floor lay a bed of mortar about 9mm (³⁄₈in) thick between the side walls. Lay the first course of bricks or blocks into this. On a timber floor, lay a strip of bitumen felt DPC (damp-proof course) across the opening, which will help to reduce noise trans-

mission. Then lay a 100 × 50mm (4 × 2in) timber sole plate over the DPC and nail it to the floor. Spread a bed of mortar on the sole plate and lay a strip of expanded metal mesh as reinforcement into the mortar. Then start laying the blocks or brickwork, trimming as necessary to match in with the existing walling.

You will develop your own technique for laying the bricks or blocks, but the usual way is to lay a bed of mortar on the previously laid course and then 'butter' with mortar the end of the brick or block to be laid before positioning it against the existing wall or previously laid brick or block.

As you build the wall, check regularly with a spirit level that the courses are horizontal and that the face of the new wall is vertical and aligned with the existing walls at each side of the opening.

When the mortar has hardened the wall is ready for plastering. Working from the bottom upwards, spread a base coat of plaster (called 'browning') over the surface using a length of wood which is long enough to span the opening to strike off the plaster layer so it is flat. Just before the plaster sets scrape off the surface so that it is about 3mm (¹⁄₈in) below the level of the surrounding plaster. Finally, when the undercoat plaster has set, skim over the entire area with finish plaster.

REMINDERS
- Have all the tools and materials you will need ready at the worksite before you start mixing mortar.
- You should have two shovels and two buckets for mixing – one of each for the dry cement.
- Mix the mortar on a hard surface outside, or on a large sheet of plywood or very thick polythene. A wall to shovel against is helpful.
- Mortar begins to 'go off' after a couple of hours. Mix only what you can use in the time.

ARCHWAYS

Arches are an attractive and elegant way to add a feeling of spaciousness to any home. An arch can be over a wide span, such as in a dividing wall where two rooms have been knocked into one to create a larger and more versatile space, or it can be on a much smaller scale as an alternative, or in addition, to a doorway – for example, leading from a dining room to a kitchen, or from a bedroom to a bathroom. Arches can also be used to enhance alcoves and create decorative openings.

An increasingly popular way of forming an arch is to use a preformed expanded metal arch frame. Various designs of these preformed arches are available, and they can be adapted to suit a wide range of opening sizes and wall thicknesses. Elliptical, Spanish and Tudor styles are ideal for wider openings, while Indian, Arabian and semicircular arches are better suited to narrower doorways.

An arch that is purely decorative and nonloadbearing can be formed in different ways. The traditional way is to make it out of plywood, chipboard or hardboard over a timber frame, or fixed direct to the walls and head of the opening.

In this case it is vital to mark out and cut the parts so they are identical or the arch will appear lopsided. Also, all the joints and the surface of the boards have to be carefully filled with plaster to form a level surface.

Finishing off can be difficult as the joint between the different materials will continually crack and unless perfectly level will show through on the surface. If the wood is painted there will be nothing to finish the wallpaper against. You can set the arch back from the face of the wall, but then it may not look like part of the structure, only an addition.

Preformed arch frames all work on more or less the same basic method. They are constructed from lightweight galvanized steel mesh, and fitting is simply a matter of nailing the frames to the walls at the top of the opening using galvanized nails and screws. The frames come in two overlapping parts, so they are suitable for use with any wall thickness.

Once the style of arch frames has been chosen, the first step is to measure the width and thickness of the unplastered opening so that the appropriate size of arch can be ordered. All styles of frames are adjustable to suit any wall thickness.

Use a piece of connecting dowel to link the bead of each section of the frame together. Then fix the front

Above: *a classic-style archway over a narrow span creates an elegant vista in this traditional, older house.*

Below: *a simple, attractive archway provides a spacious feeling in the living room, linking it with the hallway beyond.*

half of the frame to the face of the blockwork with galvanized masonry nails, making sure the frame is level. Then install the back half of the frame in the same manner.

Fasten the overlapping soffits (which form the underside of the arch) together with bright zinc-plated self-tapping screws. Twists of galvanized binding wire can also be used. Sufficient nails, screws, jointing dowels and so on are supplied with each kit. If the wall thickness is greater than 230mm (about 9in), the additional width can be made up with a strip of mesh known as a soffit strip. This is available in two widths, 150mm (6in) and 300mm (12in). Fasten the soffit strip in the same way using the self-tapping screws or galvanized binding wire.

Once the frame is nailed in position it is ready for plastering. There is a variety of plasters on the market today – traditional two-coat lightweight plaster, one-coat plaster and a number of pre-mixed DIY plasters. The latter tend to work out more expensive if large areas of plastering are to be undertaken, but for small areas they are quite economical as there will be little wastage, and they are very easy to use.

With the two-coat method, first apply a base coat of metal-lathing plaster to the frame. The diamond-shaped mesh acts as an ideal bonding surface, with the solid plaster bead giving an accurate guide to plaster depth and allowing the trowel to follow the shape. Smooth the plaster with the trowel, using the solid bead as a guide. When this is dry, a thin second coat of finish plaster is applied in the same manner.

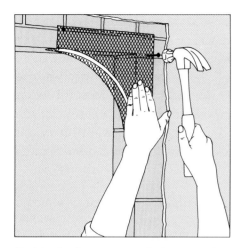

1 Mark the centre of the opening then offer one archformer to the wall and lightly nail it in place.

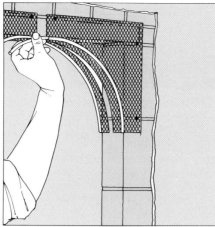

2 Insert a location jointing piece into the bead, leaving about half protruding. Fit the other archformer.

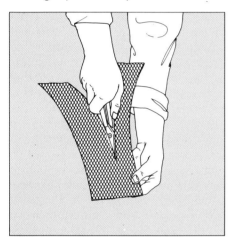

3 After fitting archformers (and bridging sections if required) cut loose soffit infill pieces to size.

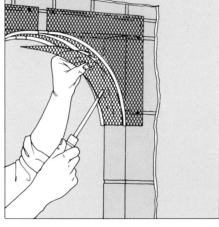

4 The soffit pieces form a continuous infill on the underside of the arch and are fitted using screws or ties.

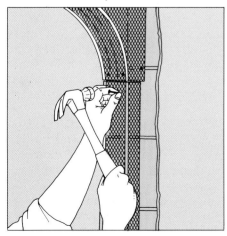

5 Nail angle bead (for brickwork) or mini-mesh angle bead (for plasterboard) on all vertical corners.

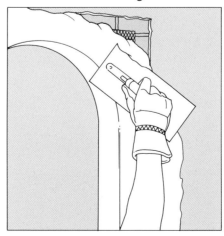

6 Plaster directly on to the steel mesh using either undercoat and finishing plasters, or one-coat plaster.

The solid bead allows the plaster to follow the shape exactly, giving a perfect and professional finish.

One-coat plaster or premixed plaster may be used and this also gives a perfect finish.

Once the plaster has thoroughly dried out it is ready for decorating. Wallpapering an arch with lining paper is straightforward. Apply the paper to each face of the arch, sealing the edge by turning a margin of paper on to the underside of the arch. Finally apply two strips of paper to the underside (or soffit) of the arch, so that they meet at the top of the arch. It is best to avoid large motifs or complicated patterns around arches since these can be very difficult to match up and can leave a very lop-sided appearance. It is easier to go for a small random pattern or use a textured paper such as a woodchip which you can then paint with emulsion.

Most of these mesh arch frames are intended for internal use, but a point to note is that arch frames are also available for external use. A selected range is available in stainless steel and in this case the arch frames are a simple and economic way of achieving aesthetically pleasing shapes, such as on verandahs, porches, gazebos, pergolas, and so on —wherever good weathering properties are required.

If you want an ornate arch in classic style, one of the best ways of achieving this effect is to use a preformed fibrous plaster arch. This type of arch is supplied in sections which are fixed to the top of the opening and, if necessary, to a light timber frame using coving adhesive. The sections can be held in place with tacks while the adhesive sets.

Often, the appearance of an arch can be greatly improved by fitting corbels at its springing points (where it originates from the side walls). Corbels are fancy plaster projections which can be formed from preformed mesh nailed to battens which are screwed to the wall, or from timber blocks or preformed fibrous plaster sections.

WALLS

There are two reasons for lining walls with sheets of plasterboard. The first is because the existing wall is sound but uneven or the plaster is in a poor state and you want to decorate using wallcovering or tiles; the second is because an outside wall is cold and you want to insulate it. The normal way of insulating cavity walls is to have the cavity filled by pumping in an insulant material. However, there is no reason why you should not use plasterboard in this situation – especially if you are only concerned about one room rather than a whole house. Most houses which were built over sixty years ago will have solid walls and here the best way you can effectively insulate from inside is to use either plasterboard or timber boards (see page 40).

The beauty of plasterboard is that it is such an easy material with which to work. You can fix it to a wall or ceiling quickly and, after you have carried out the simple job of filling the joints, the surface will be smooth and flat – equal to the most smoothly plastered surface.

You can apply most paints and wallpapers directly to the surface of the plasterboard after you have painted on a special primer/sealer.

PLASTERBOARD

The types and sizes of plasterboard are described in the chapter on materials on page 16. The main choice in size is in the thickness. 12.5mm (½in) plasterboard is more durable and requires a supporting framework at 600mm (24in) intervals. The 9.5mm (⅜in) thickness is lighter but requires support at 400mm (16in) intervals.

There are two methods of dry lining walls using plasterboard; one is to fix battens to the wall and nail the plasterboard to them and the other is to fix the plasterboard directly to the wall itself using a plaster-like adhesive.

The first method is probably the easiest for the do-it-yourself enthusiast. Battens are plugged and screwed to the wall at 600mm (24in) centres to take boards 1200mm (4ft) wide. The boards should reach from the floor to the ceiling, as the fewer joints you have the smoother the wall finish will be. Cut the boards about 6–12mm (¼–½in) short so that you can get a footlifter under them to lift them tight up to the ceiling. The small space at the bottom will be covered by the skirting board.

For dry lining, choose the type of plasterboards with tapered edges which allow a reinforcing tape and filler to be used to finish off the joint flush with the board surface. If there are any horizontal joints, you will have to fix noggings between the uprights to take the edges of these boards. It is usual to use 50 × 25mm (2 × 1in) timber for battening the walls, but where you wish to install insulation between the battens, fit thicker timber to enable more insulation to be inserted.

Where you are installing insulation, staple a vapour barrier, which could be sheet polythene, to the battens to prevent any moisture vapour penetrating the dry lining and condensing on the brick wall.

Using thermal board

Instead of using plain plasterboard on battens and filling the spaces with insulation you can use plasterboard which has its own integral insulation.

Fix it either by battening the wall or by using Gyproc multi-purpose adhesive. The board can have an integral vapour barrier and tapered edges which are finished off in the usual way.

1 Fit the first board in a corner, ensuring that it is vertical.

2 Slip a footlifter made from wood under the board to raise it into place.

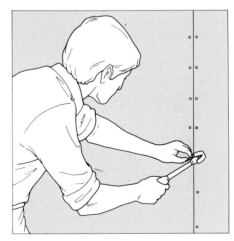

3 Nail the boards to the battens using plasterboard nails.

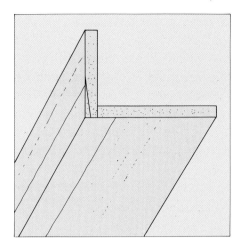

4 Fill external corners then reinforce them with corner tape covered with Jointex filler.

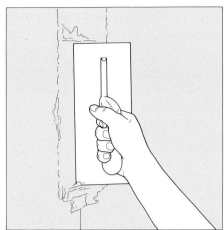

5 To fill the joints, first apply a band of Jointex to the tapered edges using a steel float.

6 Next apply joint tape, pressing it down with a filling knife so that it is well embedded in the Jointex.

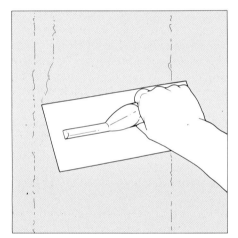

7 Use the float to apply another band of Jointex, 200mm (8in) wide.

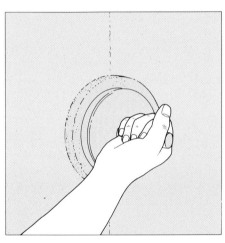

8 Feather out the edges with a moist sponge. Allow to dry.

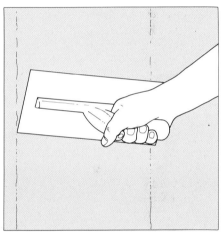

9 Finally, apply another band of Jointex, 300mm (12in) wide.

Making a footlifter

To lift a sheet of plasterboard tight against the ceiling while it is nailed to the framework you need a footlifter.

You may be able to hire one of these or you could make your own from a block of scrap wood measuring about 225 × 100 × 50mm (9 × 4 × 2in).

Clamp the block in a vice and make two angled cuts as shown to form a triangle. Push the footlifter underneath the sheet of plasterboard (the point of the triangle facing downwards) then stand on the other end to lift the board up with a minimum of effort, leaving both hands free to work.

Cutting

If you are cutting a long piece of board use a fine-tooth saw and cut ivory side up. You will need to support both pieces of the board (both sides of the cut).

Shorter pieces are easy to cut with a sharp trimming knife held against a metal straightedge; score deeply on the ivory side, snap it on a straightedge then turn the board over and cut through the paper on the grey side.

You can make cutouts for electrical sockets and switches with a pad saw. In all cases, lightly rub down cut edges with fine abrasive paper in order to remove paper burrs before you fix the boards in place.

Fixing

It takes two people to hold a board (ivory side out) against the battens. Butt the paper-covered long side edges tightly together and nail into the timbers at around 150mm (6in) centres, using galvanized plasterboard nails. Keep the nails at least 13mm (½in) away from the edges of the boards and drive them in so the large round heads just dent the surface without breaking the paper lining. Fill the holes with normal filler.

Jointing

There is more than one jointing compound for use with plasterboard but the best for the do-it-yourselfer is called Jointex. This is quick and easy to use because only one filling material is necessary.

All you need for filling the joints between boards is the jointing compound and jointing tape. For external angles, it is sensible to reinforce with corner tape, which is paper tape with two metal strips. This is sold in rolls.

Use the same tape for the joint between the top of the boards and the ceiling or use plaster or fix a cove or cornice. The gap between the bottom of the boards and the floor is not important because it will be covered by skirting boards.

PLASTERING

Although most people are not likely to attempt to plaster a whole room, you may want to repair a large patch where a window, door or fireplace has been blocked off. For such a job it is easy for the beginner to achieve a smooth, flat finish with either a ready-to-use DIY plaster or a traditional type. Preparation for plastering must be thorough. Remove all loose and flaking plaster and if the reason for the plaster failure was dampness then you must find the cause and cure it, otherwise your new patch will fail in the same way.

Once you have cleaned off all the loose material, wet the wall and apply the plaster. When you have applied an undercoat about 12mm (½in) thick, use a fairly wide straightedge to level off the plaster by working it up the wall with a sawing action.

The undercoat should finish about 3mm (⅛in) below the surrounding plaster so that you can apply a finishing plaster flush with the original wall surface.

When you are smoothing the finish plaster, you may use a little water but do not over wet it or the final, dried surface will be dusty.

Types of plaster

The two main types of plaster you are likely to need around the house are Carlite and Thistle. Each type is applied in two layers – first an

1 Use a wood or plastic float to apply the undercoat; work upwards.

2 Draw a wood straightedge upwards to level the surface.

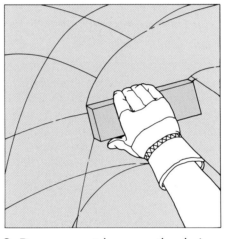

3 Draw a scratcher over the drying undercoat to key the surface.

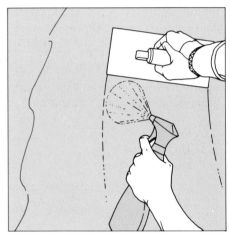

4 A steel float and light spraying gives a fine finish to the top coat.

undercoat (called Browning) and then a finishing layer.

Carlite is a lightweight plaster which is premixed – you need only add water. After applying the undercoat, scratch the surface to form a key for the finishing coat of Carlite Finish. You can apply this as soon as the undercoat has set, which takes 1½ to 2 hours.

Use only clean water for mixing the plaster. Clean the mixing platform or bucket after each mix as any set plaster left over from the previous mix will reduce the setting time of the next and could also weaken it.

Thistle plaster

Thistle Browning is mixed with

sand, usually to a ratio of one part plaster to three parts sand. It must be thoroughly mixed dry before the water is added. As with the Carlite, the Browning should be about 12mm (½in) thick and applied in two coats. The Browning must be scratched before the finishing coat is applied.

Mix Thistle Finish in a clean bucket, adding the plaster to the water and stirring thoroughly all the time to prevent lumps occurring.

DIY plasters

Special plasters have been developed for DIY use. These require no undercoat and you can apply them up to about 50mm (2in) thick directly on to brickwork or similar walls without the sagging you would get with traditional plasters if they were applied at that thickness in one coat. However, they are more expensive than traditional plasters.

One ready-mixed, lightweight, grey-coloured plaster has the advantage of being suitable for either indoors or outdoors. You can apply it with a trowel or filling knife up to 50mm (2in) thick and if you need a greater thickness you can build it up in layers.

Strike it off level with the surrounding surface and smooth it off to a fine finish. As the material stays workable for quite a long period, you have plenty of time to bring it to a satisfactory finish. When it is completely dry you can decorate it in the same way as conventional plaster.

Another ready-mixed plaster gives a skim finish. This is ideal for levelling rough surfaces. It is brush applied, or you can use the spreader given in the packs, to no more than

3mm (⅛in) thickness.

You can use it on plaster, plasterboard, bricks or blocks and you have plenty of time before it sets to bring it to a good finish. It dries to a white finish in about 24 hours, when it is ready for decorating.

Mix it yourself

Another type is a powder that is easily mixed with water. It comes in three separate bags packed in a plastic bucket which is marked with the correct water levels for one, two or three bag mixes, and in smaller packs with or without the plastic bucket. You can apply the plaster up to 50mm (2in) thick and feather it off to finish it smoothly with the existing plaster. Both the thick and the thin areas will set at the same slow pace so that you have plenty of time to obtain a smooth finish, for which you can use a damp sponge.

If large areas are to be covered

with any type of plaster, it is a good idea to nail guide battens to the wall temporarily so that you can use a straightedge to bring all the plastered surface to the same level. You can remove the battens later and fill the grooves they have made level with the rest of the work.

Tools

A trowel is ideal for mixing the plaster and for carrying out small repairs, although many people prefer to fill cracks with a filling knife.

You will need two floats – a wooden or plastic one for the undercoat to make a rough finish and a metal one to achieve a smooth surface with the finishing plaster. Use a straightedge piece of wood to level the undercoat roughly.

You will also need a hawk to carry the plaster from the mixing point to the wall and if you hold the hawk against the wall you will be able to

1A Provided that the laths are still solid, holes in a lath and plaster wall can be filled as for solid walls. Reinforce broken laths with expanded metal mesh stapled in place.

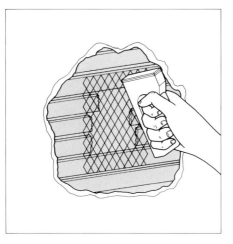

2A A corner needs to be reinforced for repair. Here angle bead is held in blobs of plaster set at 300mm (12in) spaces.

1B Apply two coats of plaster – an undercoat followed by a finishing coat.

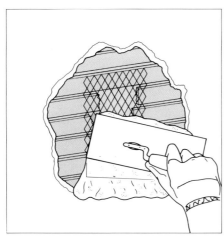

2B Plaster the two walls in turn, working away from the corner and leaving the 'nose' of the angle bead just visible.

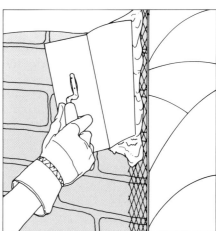

catch most of the droppings.

You will require a small hand sprayer or 100mm (4in) wall brush to damp the wall and a scratcher to score the undercoat and provide a key for the finishing coat.

Store plaster in dry conditions otherwise it will deteriorate quickly. Keep it covered and off the ground if it is in a garage or shed. Keep partly used bags in a sealed plastic bag.

CLADDING

Tongued and grooved boarding looks naturally warm and attractive and is extremely practical. It can cover up a poor wall surface in an old house; it lowers a ceiling or hides a damaged one; it can be used to box in pipes in a kitchen or bathroom. Wood is a natural insulator, the boards are very easy to put up and, once finished with a seal or varnish, they are easy to keep clean.

Types of boards

There are three main types of tongued and grooved boards; narrow V, wide V and shiplap. The narrow V is by far the commonest. They are usually pine or cedar (hardwood types can be expensive) and they are 100mm (4in) wide, which covers only 88mm (3½in) because the tongue fits inside the groove.

Damp

If there is any sign of damp on the wall you wish to cover, you must solve that problem first before fixing battens and boards.

Architraves and skirtings

Using a cold chisel and a club hammer, prise off all door and window architraves so that they can be replaced later for a neat and even appearance.

Leave skirting boards in position so they can be used as a bottom fixing; if the skirting is thinner than the wall battens being used, you will have to pack it out a bit.

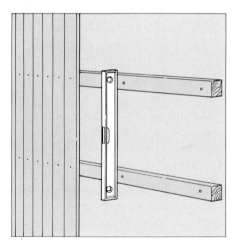

1 Battens fixed to the wall provide a level surface on which to mount the boards.

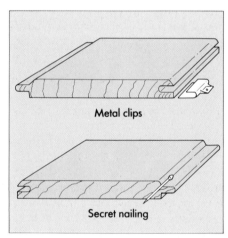

2 Two methods of fixing the boards – using pins or metal clips. Both are concealed by the next board.

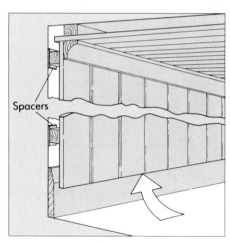

3 Methods of finishing at skirting and ceiling (with moulding) to allow airflow, with spacers behind battens.

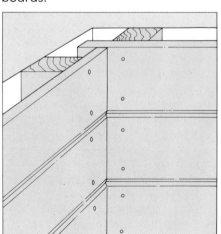

4 The boards can be simply butt joined at corners or covered with moulding.

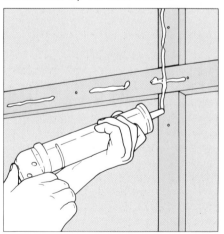

5 For fixing wallboards, adhesive is used in long vertical strips and short horizontal strips.

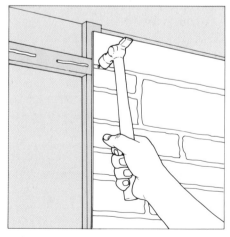

6 Wallboards should be lightly pinned at the top until the adhesive has set firmly.

For a neat finish, a batten or moulding can be fixed to the bottom sawn edges of the boards – it is best to leave a small gap of around 3mm (⅛in) at the bottom for ventilation.

Fixing the battens

Fix the wall battens vertically if the tongued and grooved boards are to be horizontal and vice versa. Fix them at 500mm (20in) centres and use 50 × 25mm (2 × 1in) softwood – sawn (unplaned) battens are more economical.

When fixing wall battens horizontally, it is a good idea to place some packing pieces (hardboard or plywood would do) between the battens and the wall at the fixing points so air can flow up and down in the space behind the boarding.

Fixing the boards

The cheapest way to fix the boards is to use panel pins driven at an angle through the base of the tongues. You need a nail punch of the correct size to punch the pinheads below the surface of the timber so the next board's groove fits over it. This is called 'secret nailing' because the nailheads cannot be seen when the job is finished. Take care not to split the tongue when punching the heads below the surface; use panel pins or oval nails to reduce the risk of this.

The alternative is to use purpose-made metal fixing clips which slide into the groove of the boards, securing them to the battens.

You will have to plane the tongue or groove off both boards where they meet at an internal or external corner. Use a sharp plane so that there is no gap once the boards are fixed.

When you are boarding over the position of an existing wall switch, you can either leave the switch where it is and form a lipped recess in the new wall surface, or move the switch to the surface.

Use brass screws and screw cups to fix boards when boxing in water pipes, or panelling a bath or sink, so that you can gain access easily should you ever need to.

In humid areas fix the boards ver-

Above: *t&g cladding has been used here for warmth and continuity.*

tically so water can run down without getting stuck in the joins. Do not fix the boards too tightly together (they need room for expansion and contraction) and make sure there is ventilation behind the boarding.

Stop the boards short of a work surface which is likely to get wet from time to time (the gap can be sealed with a nonsetting mastic).

Decorative wallboards

Decorative wallboards, 2400 × 1200mm (8 × 4ft), are available in a range of designs – various woodgrains, ceramic tiles or brickwork effects. Once fixed, the boards are maintenance-free apart from an occasional wipe over with a damp cloth.

Use adhesive to stick the boards directly to smooth walls or fix battens to the wall first and glue the boards to them. Use the latter method where walls are uneven as the battens can be packed straight and true so that the finished panelling is flat.

Fix horizontal battens at 400mm (16in) centres and vertical battens at 1200mm (4ft) centres. Apply a continuous ribbon of adhesive to the battens around the outer edge of the panels with 75mm (3in) strips of adhesive 150mm (6in) apart along the horizontal battens.

Use small packings to ensure that the panels have the required 6mm (¼in) clearance at the top and bottom for ventilation. Tack the tops of the panels lightly to hold them until the adhesive attains full grip, then press the panels against the wall again after about 15 minutes to ensure complete contact with the adhesive.

When you are fixing directly to the wall it is important that the surface is clean. Sand painted walls to provide a roughened finish so that the glue can grip.

Cut the boards with a fine-toothed panel saw to reduce the raggedness at the back of the cut. You can plane this woolly edge off if the plane cutter is really sharp. The alternative is to use abrasive paper, but this does not leave a sharp edge to the board.

CEILINGS

A ceiling may not be the most dominant feature in a room, but it has a decided effect on its appearance, and can make a big difference to what it costs to heat the room. A lowered ceiling, for example, will reduce the volume of air in the room which has to be heated, and wood cladding reduces the amount of heat lost through the ceiling and cuts down condensation.

Lowering a ceiling and cladding it in wood also gives you the chance to improve the lighting in the room, doing away with a single central pendant perhaps, and instead fitting downlights, spotlights or track lighting as you wish.

A few words of warning if the old ceiling is badly cracked or sagging. Probe the ceiling and pull away the loose parts – if you find you end up removing all the old ceiling plaster at least the messy part of the job is out of the way, and you may simply want to replace the ceiling with sheets of plasterboard nailed to the ceiling joists.

LOWERING A CEILING

There may be several reasons for wanting to lower a ceiling, but the main ones are to make the room more cosy and easier to heat, and also to hide an ugly ceiling which may be cracked or have water pipes on the surface. More than likely the ceiling in question will be in a tall room and you will want to lower it by a significant amount, but remember that it is not always essential to do so. If you just want to cover an ugly ceiling you may want to build the new ceiling just a few inches below the existing one, and this is perfectly acceptable.

In fact, it is important not to lower a ceiling too much. Building Regulations require that the underside of a ceiling must be at least 2.3m (7ft 6in) above the floor and it is best to aim to have the ceiling 2.4m (8ft) high. It is also important not to cover up windows, which would reduce ventilation.

For effective sound and heat insulation it is best to lower the ceiling by building a substantial timber frame below the existing ceiling to which sheets of plasterboard or tongued and grooved timber boarding (called matching) can be fixed. The resulting surface will be indistinguishable from a conventional ceiling.

However, if you are happy with a tiled effect, and you are only lowering the ceiling to hide pipes and an ugly old ceiling, then you may prefer to fit a lightweight suspended ceiling. This comprises lightweight metal angle sections which are fitted to the perimeter walls and across the ceiling to form a simple grid. Between the grid sections ceiling tiles are positioned and these may be lightweight plastic, which can be illuminated from above, or fibre board if more effective insulation is required (see overleaf).

Most people, however, will prefer to have the traditional lowered ceiling which we show here. The first step is to build the structure that will support the new ceiling. The ceiling will be heavy and so this needs to be substantial. Use 75 × 50mm (3 × 2in) sawn timber for the new ceiling joists, which should be cut to span the room across its shortest width. These joists should be spaced 400mm (16in) apart. At

Above: Spaced square-edged battens used to lower a high ceiling.

each side they should rest on timber bearers of 75 × 50mm (3 × 2in) which are fixed to the wall surface about 9.5mm (⅜in) – the thickness of the plasterboard – above the desired height for the new ceiling. At each end of the room, the timber frame around the perimeter of the wall is completed with a 50 × 25mm (2 × 1in) batten which is also screwed to the wall surface.

Start by deciding at what height you want the ceiling and, allowing for the thickness of the plasterboard or timber to be used to cover the ceiling, draw a horizontal line right around the perimeter of the room at this height. On each end wall, drill,

plug, and screw a 50 × 25mm batten to the wall so that the lower edge of the batten touches the marked line. On the longer, opposite walls, the 75 × 50mm bearers will be fixed. Cut these to length, then notch their ends so they will rest on the battens with their lower edges flush with them. Before fixing these bearers, cut halvings (notches) in the bearers of 400mm (16in) centres to match similar halvings to be cut in the ends of the support joists which will be fitted across the room.

Before fitting these joists, screw a 75 × 50mm bearer to the ceiling running the length of the room at approximately the midpoint of the

ceiling. Fit the joists into the bearers and check that the undersides are flush with the undersides of the bearers. Nail the joists in place and then fit 75 × 50mm (3 × 2in) or 50 × 50mm (2 × 2in) hangers between the ceiling-bearer and the sides of the joists to support them about their mid-point. These hangers are required only if the room width is more than 2.4m (8ft).

All that remains is to fit the cladding material. If you are using plasterboard, start in one corner of the room and fix the first sheet so its long length is at right angles to the direction of the ceiling joists. If necessary trim the sheet so its end

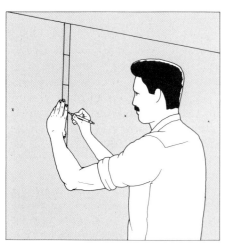

1 Mark the height for the lowered ceiling on the wall. Mark a horizontal line all round.

2 At each end of the room screw and plug a 50 × 25mm (2 × 1in) horizontal batten to the wall.

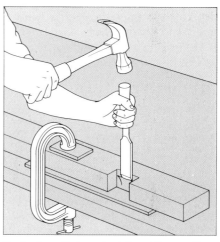

3 Before fixing the 75 × 50mm (3 × 2in) wall bearers cut notches at 400mm (16in) centres for the joists.

4 Notch the ends of the wall bearers to rest on the end battens, then screw the bearers to the wall.

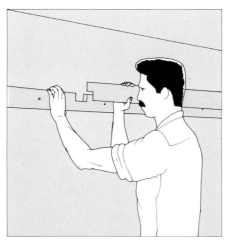

5 The ceiling joists are also notched at their ends and then fitted into the bearers.

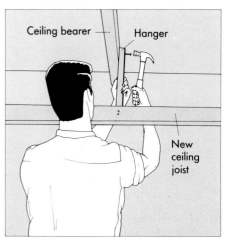

6 Finish the framework ready for cladding by nailing hangers between a ceiling bearer and the joists.

falls midway across a ceiling joist then nail it in place using galvanized, large-head plasterboard nails. Fit the board cream side downwards so it will be ready for direct decoration. Cut subsequent sheets of plasterboard so that the joints between the ends of the sheets do *not* line up. For a neat finish around the edge of the room, fit plaster coving.

If you choose to fit a lightweight suspended ceiling, there are several kits on the market which use lightweight metal angle sections to form a grid below the ceiling, and into which the grid tiles are fixed. Often these are thin, translucent plastic which allow light to shine through from fluorescent tubes fixed to the original ceiling, or fibre tiles can be fitted into the grid.

To fit a ceiling of this type, start by nailing or screwing edge-trim sections horizontally to the walls at the required ceiling height. Across the shorter width of the room, main tee-sections are cut and these rest on the previously-fixed edge-trim sections. Space these main tee-sections carefully so they will support the ceiling panels and give evenly sized cut border tiles around the perimeter of the ceiling. Next, cut cross tee-sections to fit between the main tee-sections to build up the grid formation. The panels rest in the grid and hold the sections evenly apart.

CLADDING

Normally, ceilings are clad in tongued, grooved and V-jointed boards called 'matching', available in various widths and styles. You can also use plain (square-edge) boards, and there are various ways of fixing these in an overlapping fashion to form wide or narrow recesses which can be accentuated by using boards of different widths. Alternatively, a single layer of square-edge boards can be fixed with regular spaces between them so that the background shows through.

It is usual to fix cladding close to the original ceiling, but if you want to lower the ceiling you can do this

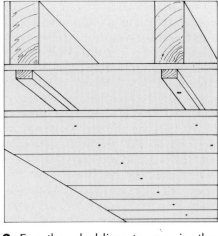

1 Timber matching pinned to battens screwed at right angles to the run of the ceiling joists.

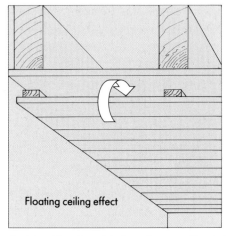

2 For the cladding to run in the other direction, the battens can be fixed in line with the joists.

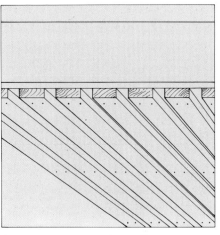

3 For an interesting effect, square-edge boards can be fixed direct to the ceiling with gaps between.

Floating ceiling effect

4 Ideal for humid situations, a floating ceiling effect allows air to circulate behind the boards.

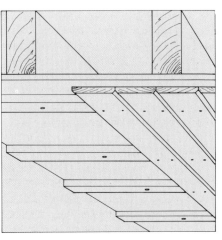

5 Three interesting effects that can be created by overlapping square-edge boards.

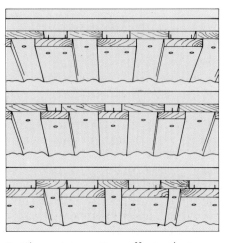

6 Fixing boards to ceilings; a: face-fixing with screws; b: hidden fixing clips; c: secret nailing.

by building a timber framework as described on the previous page.

If the ceiling is flat, level, and in reasonably good condition, it is possible to fix the cladding direct to the ceiling surface. However, it is best to screw the boards to the ceiling in this case, to minimize the risk of bringing down the ceiling when fixing the boards. Such a method is particularly suitable for square-edge boards being fixed with gaps between the boards. Paint the ceiling black first and make a feature of the fixing screws (by using brassed screws, say) which are driven through the ceiling and into the ceiling joists. To locate the ceiling joists, which are normally spaced 400mm (16in) apart, use an electronic joist and stud detector, or a metal detec-

tor which locates the nails used to fix the plasterboard. Alternatively, probe the ceiling to find them. Draw lines on the ceiling to indicate the run of the joists.

Usually it is best to fix the boards to a series of battens which are first screwed to the ceiling at right angles to the run of the cladding boards. Screw the battens to the joists, spacing them from 400 to 610mm (16 to 24in) apart. The battens should be 38mm (1½in) wide by 25mm (1in) thick and you can put packing pieces under them if necessary to produce a flat undersurface.

Fix the timber boards using either special fixing clips or by pinning, using the technique called 'secret' nailing. This involves driving a pin at an angle through the board at the

shoulder of the tongue so it is not seen when the next board is fitted. However, it is easy to split the boards in this way and to avoid this use fixing clips which are simply nailed to the battens. Of course, you can face-fix the boards with screws or nails if preferred, but this must be done in neat lines.

Normally the boards are taken to within about 6mm (¼in) of the walls to allow for movement in the wood, and the gap is concealed by pinning a narrow timber scotia or quadrant moulding to the *wall*. However, in kitchens and bathrooms, where conditions will be humid, it is best to stop the battens and the cladding about 50mm (2in) short of the walls, to allow for ventilation behind the cladding.

LIGHTING

Downlighters These are fitted into the ceiling so that the bottom edge of the fitting is flush with the surface of the ceiling. The downlighter casts a beam downwards, creating a pool of light below the fitting. Because the light is not spread far it is common to fit a line of downlighters to produce a 'curtain' of light.
Eyeball fittings and wallwashers These are a variation on the downlighter theme. They are recessed into the ceiling, but the lighting is adjustable. With an eyeball fitting, the lamp can be swivelled to almost

any angle and it is usually fitted with a spotlight to direct light on to a particular object or feature. With a wallwasher, the fitting directs light in a wider beam to illuminate a feature on a wall.
Track lighting This is a very versatile system that allows various types of light fitting to be clipped anywhere on a ceiling-mounted track. Spotlights, floodlights and more diffused lights up to the maximum wattage stated by the manufacturer can be clipped into the track.
Pendant lights The traditional

Above: eyeball downlighter, pendant, spotlights, track lighting and fluorescents – modern ceiling lights come in wide variety.

form of lighting, but they need not be confined to the centre of the ceiling. They have the advantage of making a high ceiling seem lower and can be sited over a dining table where a rise-and-fall fitting with a directional shade can be useful especially if combined with a dimmer switch.

WARDROBES

The big advantage of a fitted wardrobe over a freestanding one is that it makes the best use of the available space – it can be taken right up to the ceiling and right up to a wall, sometimes to both walls to produce wall-to-wall cupboards. Not only does this provide maximum storage space, but it also means that the wardrobe looks much more attractive.

There are basically four ways of achieving fitted wardrobes. First you can use modular bedroom furniture units – wardrobes, drawer units, dressing tables, and so on – which are linked together in much the same way as kitchen units. This is not a cheap option, and the units may not meet your needs exactly. Only custom-built systems can achieve this and they form the second option: buy the components in kit form, or as cupboard fronts.

Wardrobe kits contain all you need for making a fitted wardrobe – door panels, door track, and interior fittings such as shelves, drawers and hanging rails. Cupboard fronts are usually factory-assembled and consist of a complete frame with hinged doors already hung in place.

The third method, particularly suitable for alcoves or where an entire wall is to be covered, is to buy sliding or bi-fold door gear together with doors and cover the entire space from floor to ceiling, using hanging rails and other internal fitments behind.

Finally, you can make the whole wardrobe yourself by fitting a timber frame with hinged, sliding or bi-fold doors. You can add top cupboards in high rooms and end panels where the wardrobe does not fit in an alcove or wall-to-wall.

Sliding mirror doors are ideal on wardrobes in restricted spaces

Have a good look at the bedroom at the planning stage to avoid running into problems later. It is easy, for instance, to overlook an electric socket or a radiator, or to forget to allow for the position of a door or window. Allow at least 700mm (2ft 3in) between the wardrobe front and the bed so as to allow you to make the bed and clean the carpet. When choosing doors remember that hinged types encroach quite heavily over the floor space; the wider the door the more space it needs. You can save space by using bi-fold (folding) doors which have the advantage that they fully reveal the contents of the wardrobe when opened. Mirrored, louvred, and panelled bi-fold doors are available, but a little more care and adjustment is required in fitting than with ordinary hinged or sliding doors.

Probably the most versatile wardrobe system can be found with large sliding doors, particularly mirror doors, which are ideal where space is restricted because the reflections created by full length mirrors make the room seem much larger. If you do not want mirror sliding doors, there are plenty of white and wood-effect panel doors and if your budget is small you can use veneered plywood or chipboard.

If possible, arrange for the hanging rail to run from side to side in the wardrobe so you can see the clothes at a glance. In this case the front-to-back depth of the wardrobe should be about 610mm (2ft), which will allow the clothes to hang without scuffing on the rear wall or on the doors. This depth will also allow you to use standard-size 2440 × 610mm (8 × 2ft) cut sheets of faced chipboard to make the two end panels without wastage.

If there is not the space to allow the wardrobe to be this deep, there are 'fore-and-aft' hanging rails which pull forwards to make clothes selection easier. However, do make sure that the wardrobe is not so narrow that it will not take standard interior fittings.

At the design and planning stage, probably the single most important tool required will be a 1m (3ft) spirit level used in conjunction with a 1.5 or 1.8m (5 or 6ft) long straightedge, and a steel measuring tape.

You will need these tools for checking the squareness of the opening and the flatness of walls and ceiling. It is best to assume that the walls, floor and ceiling are out of square, as they almost certainly will be. For hinged and sliding doors to close properly it is *vital* that the framework of the wardrobe is square, and you will have to use packing pieces to square the framework and cover strips to hide any gaps this causes.

By placing the spirit level on top of the straightedge held flush against the wall, ceiling and floor line at various points you will be able to establish where the surround is out of true and where packing is likely to be needed. This will also enable you to establish the narrowest width and the shortest floor-to-ceiling height. These are the dimensions you must work to. For example, if a recess is 1220mm (48in) wide at the front and 1232mm (48⅓in) wide at the back, it is the smallest dimension that must be used as the basis for the design. Similarly, it is the shortest floor-to-ceiling height that must be used for the overall frame height, which in turn fixes the door height.

Other on-site problems are picture rails and skirting boards. You must either scribe (shape) the side frames

BUILDING A WARDROBE IN A RECESS

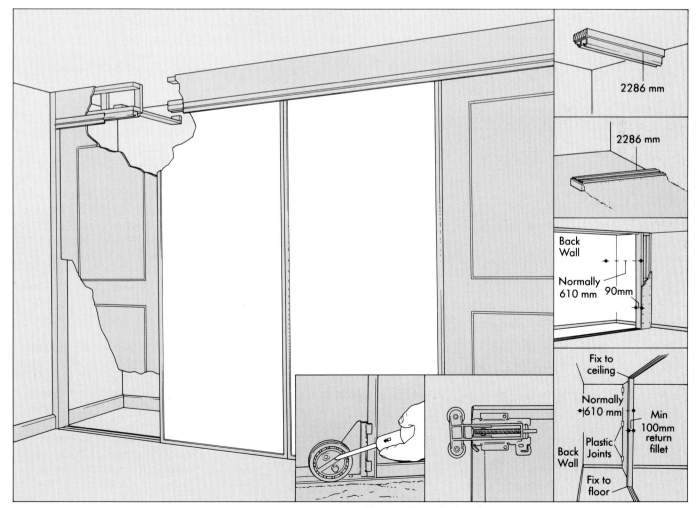

Using a panel or mirror door wardrobe kit makes it easy to fit a wall-to-wall wardrobe.

BUILDING A WARDROBE ON A FLUSH WALL

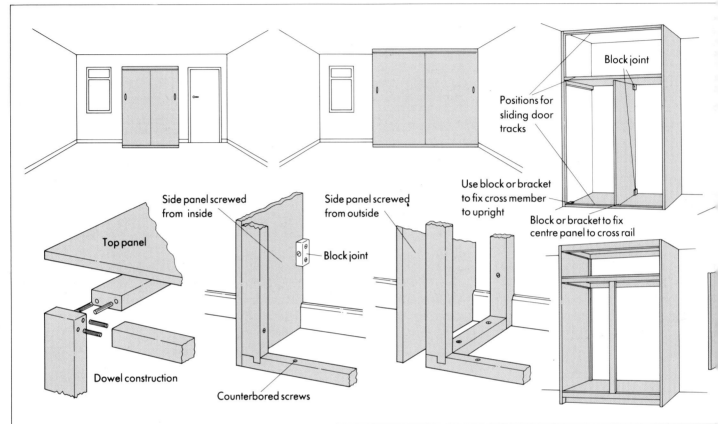

Block joint

Positions for sliding door tracks

Top panel

Side panel screwed from inside

Block joint

Side panel screwed from outside

Use block or bracket to fix cross member to upright

Block or bracket to fix centre panel to cross rail

Dowel construction

Counterbored screws

to go over them or simply trim them off to accommodate the side frames. Also, use a metal detector to check for underfloor pipes and cables before making floor fixings.

Overcoming problems

When you are working from scratch, as long as you build your framework absolutely square and vertical, then you should not have too many problems to overcome with regard to fitting the framework into the opening. You are free to make the frame and the doors to any size required.

Most cupboard fronts and wardrobe kits are, however, made to a limited range of sizes and there may be some making-up required to reduce the opening width and height to suit your needs.

With cupboard fronts, the projections on the frame must be reduced to match the height of the room. Take your measurements with care, and do not be surprised to find small differences in floor/ceiling distances.

Thin timber wedges are needed when the assembly is offered up. Then you must carry out some rigorous checks with a spirit level to make sure that the frame members are exactly vertical when viewed from each face.

Do not be tempted to level up horizontal frame members against the floor or ceiling. Again, make checks with a spirit level and insert small packing pieces of thin plywood or hardboard under the feet until the frame is correct. It is not unusual to have a gentle slope in a floor but you must not let this be reflected in the framework.

When you are certain that the framework is square and plumb, you should then anchor the feet permanently by driving an angled woodscrew directly into the floorboards. A similar anchorage is needed at the ceiling, but plasterwork does not give a suitable fixing. If you make small holes with a bradawl, inspection from above indicates the pos-

ition of the joists and the place where you need to fix a timber nogging (batten) on top of the ceiling. Of course, you may be lucky enough to find a joist for the fixing screw but do not worry if you need to add some support/timber. It largely depends on whether the top member of the framework will run at right angles to or be parallel with the joists. If at right angles then it should not be necessary to add noggings to serve as screw fixing points.

When fitting a sliding door wardrobe kit it is often necessary to reduce the width of the opening slightly. If you need to reduce the width by less than 150mm (6in) fix a length of timber at least 100mm (4in) wide and up to 75mm (3in) thick on each side of the opening.

If you need to reduce the width of the opening by more than 150mm (6in), build panels at each side of the opening from two lengths of 100 × 50mm (4 × 2in) timber and face these with plywood or chipboard. An

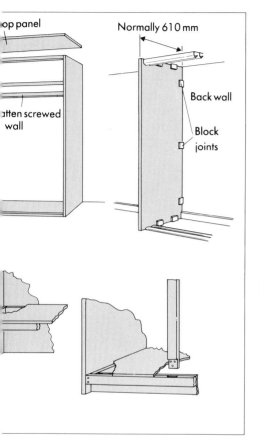

op panel

Normally 610 mm

atten screwed
wall

Back wall

Block
joints

Left: on a flush
wall, a wardrobe
can be built in a
corner, requiring
one end panel, or
on a flat wall,
when two end
panels are
required.

Above: louvred
doors used on a
floor-to-ceiling
corner wardrobe.

Below: it is
important to get a
secure fixing when
mounting door
track or the
wardrobe frame
on a ceiling. Screw
directly into the
ceiling joists, or fit

battens between
the joists to take
the fixing screws.
Some wardrobe
kits allow the track
to be fitted direct
to the ceiling
plasterboard using
cavity fixings.

SIMPLE JOINTS FOR WARDROBE PANELS

CEILING FIXINGS

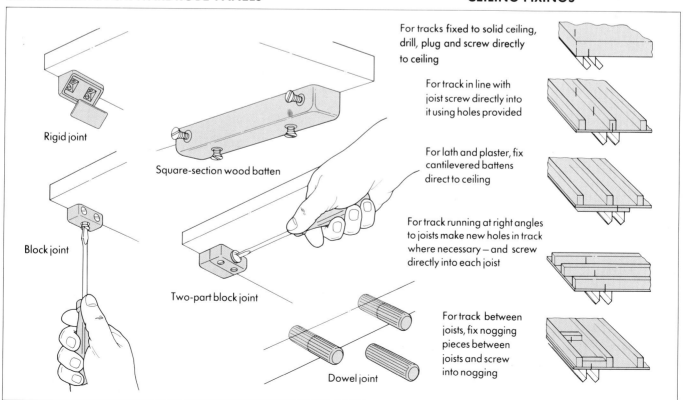

Rigid joint

Block joint

Square-section wood batten

Two-part block joint

Dowel joint

For tracks fixed to solid ceiling,
drill, plug and screw directly
to ceiling

For track in line with
joist screw directly into
it using holes provided

For lath and plaster, fix
cantilevered battens
direct to ceiling

For track running at right angles
to joists make new holes in track
where necessary – and screw
directly into each joist

For track between
joists, fix nogging
pieces between
joists and screw
into nogging

alternative is to frame the wardrobe opening in the normal way, and leave the side frame member away from the wall by an equal amount on each side to suit the doors being used. Then fill the gap between the frame and the door with veneer or melamine-faced chipboard fixed with plastic block joint fittings.

It is often necessary to fit an end panel to seal one end of a wardrobe. You can easily make this panel from a sheet of blockboard or chipboard, suitably veneered, cut to fit between floor and ceiling height. Scribe the back edge of the panel to fit against the rear wall and skirting and fit it in place using plastic joint blocks equally spread around the top, back and bottom.

Most sliding mirror door wardrobe kits are made to fit standard 2.29m (90in) high ceiling heights and if your floor-to-ceiling height is within 12mm (½in) of this you can screw the track directly to the floor and ceiling. (The better quality door kits have a spring-loaded top guide on the doors which automatically compensates if the ceiling is up to 12mm (½in) out of true.) If you have a plasterboard ceiling in good condition it is possible to fit the track to the ceiling using cavity fixings direct into the plasterboard. If the ceiling is out of true, you should fit the track to a suitably packed-out timber batten.

If the ceiling height is over 2.29m (90in) you can either fit the top track to a ceiling batten of suitable thickness, or, if there is a considerable gap, fit it to a box beam from two timber battens covered in plywood at front and back.

Non-mirror sliding door wardrobe kits will normally fit a wider range of opening sizes. After measuring the size of the opening, cut the door tracks and door framing to suit following the fitting instructions supplied. Saw the doors to size and conceal the cut edges with the door framing, which clips into place. Fit the top and bottom tracks, fit out the interior then hang the doors and adjust them to glide smoothly.

Interior fitments

Fitted wardrobes help you make the best use of space, but they must be fitted out carefully inside or you will end up with an unkempt jumble.

It is a good idea to fit an intermediate shelf to the width of the wardrobe just above hanging rail height with a clearance of 45–62mm (1¾–2½in) to allow space for coat hangers to be hooked over the rail.

You can make the shelf from melamine-faced chipboard and simply fix it inside the wardrobe using plastic block joint fittings. A narrow plinth attached to the underside front edge of the shelf (also by block joints) will stiffen the shelf and at the same time hide the fixings.

Where the wardrobe is not sufficiently deep for a side-to-side rail there are various extending front-to-back rails which enable you to pick out clothes easily.

Melamine-faced chipboard is ideal for making shelf and drawer storage units for inside a wardrobe, or you can buy various ready-made sliding plastic tray and wire basket storage fittings.

Hinges, sliding door gear, catches

There are many types of hinges for wardrobe doors. If the wardrobe is a simple two-door veneered chipboard type with lay-on doors (where the door covers the side pieces), then you can use inexpensive flush hinges. These need no recessing; they just screw to the edge or face of the door and side frame using chipboard-type screws. Three hinges are required per wardrobe door.

Use single or double cranked hinges to hang the doors where they

INTERIOR FITTINGS

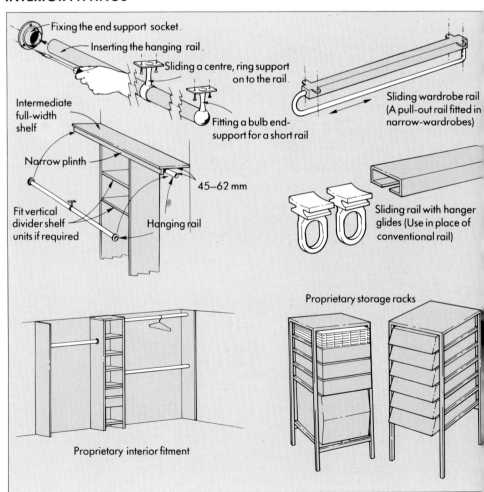

Fixing the end support socket.
Inserting the hanging rail.
Sliding a centre, ring support on to the rail.
Intermediate full-width shelf
Fitting a bulb end-support for a short rail
Sliding wardrobe rail (A pull-out rail fitted in narrow-wardrobes)
Narrow plinth
45–62 mm
Fit vertical divider shelf units if required
Hanging rail
Sliding rail with hanger glides (Use in place of conventional rail)
Proprietary storage racks
Proprietary interior fitment

may get rough use. The crank gives a little extra support to the door.

Once fitted, these flush hinges are not adjustable, so for this reason it is common to fit concealed hinges on wardrobes with hinged doors. The advantage here is that all concealed hinges are adjustable so it is easy to get the doors to hang exactly level with each other, and if the frame or carcass of the wardrobe is slightly out of true, this can be allowed for.

Other advantages of concealed hinges are that they throw the doors clear of the carcass when opened and on a wide wardrobe they allow doors to be hinged together on a common centre panel without the doors fouling each other when you open them together.

The standard concealed hinge opens the door in a 100° arc, but if you want better access to the inside fitments, then 125° versions are available. If you want the doors to fold right back against adjoining doors, choose the 170° versions.

You can also have these hinges sprung or unsprung. Sprung hinges are more expensive, but they hold the doors closed without the need for separate catches.

Lay-on concealed hinges are simply screwed to the inside faces of the doors, but for a neater and stronger fitting it is best to use recessed hinges where the hinge is fitted in a blind (shallow) hole drilled in the rear face of the door. Screw the appropriate base plate to the carcass side, and secure the hinge to the base plate with a single screw to hang the door. Another screw allows adjustment for a perfect fit. To drill the blind hole an end mill (also called a hinge sinker) is required. For accuracy in drilling this is best fitted into an electric drill mounted in a drill stand.

For sliding doors, single and twin track is available. The doors usually hang from the top track and the bottom track simply guides them. In all cases the track screws to the ceiling or to a timber bearer fitted across the top of the opening.

Bi-fold doors also hang from a top track, but in this case the outer door is fitted in pivots and the inner door of each pair is hinged to the outer door, as shown in the drawing.

Below: *in a DIY wardrobe it is a good idea to fit a full-width shelf at eye level which will support a hanging rail screwed to its underside using rail support brackets. A plinth running the length of the shelf will help to prevent it from sagging over wide spans – or fit vertical dividers for extra support.*

HINGES AND SLIDING DOOR GEAR

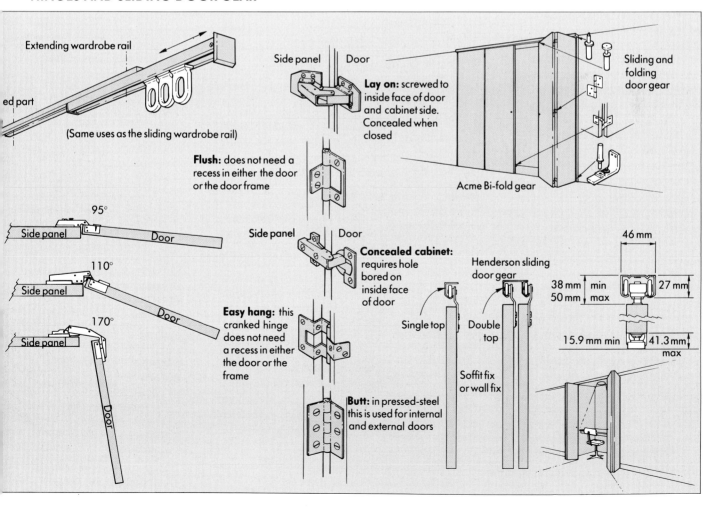

FIREPLACES

Fireplaces are back in fashion with open fires to create focal points in living rooms. Much of the renewed popularity of the open fire must be due to the modern gas-burning coal-effect and log-effect fires which look realistic but do not create the mess that goes hand-in-hand with a 'real' fire.

If you live in a house where the fireplaces have been blocked up you may well want to open them up again so that you can use the flue and chimney.

If you live in a house built without chimneys, there is nothing to stop you from building a fireplace with an imitation fire, or fitting a sealed balanced-flue gas fire that does not require a chimney. Otherwise you will have to install a modular, sectional fireplace opening connected to a lightweight pre-formed flue or chimney, which must be taken up well above the roof line either externally or within the house.

Above left: a simple, rustic-looking fireplace built of rough-hewn stone.

Above right: attractive modern version of the traditional wood and tiled surround.

Left: a Burbridge fireplace with elegant Regency-style wood surround

Opening a flue and removing a fireplace

Assuming a house has been built with chimneys which are not used at present, reinstatement must start with opening a sealed flue, or removing an unwanted fireplace.

Openings are usually sealed with bricks or blocks, with an airbrick to provide gentle ventilation of the flue, or they may be boarded up with plasterboard or a similar non-combustible sheet material on a timber frame. To unblock this type of opening, use a cold chisel and club hammer to break away the bricks or blocks, and a wrecking bar or similar lever to pull away any boards and their framework. An accumulation of soot indicates that the chimney should be swept, which you should arrange to have done before proceeding. A small amount of mortar in the opening is no cause for concern, but if there is a considerable amount of rubble and mortar, get a builder to look at the condition of the flue and chimney stack before proceeding.

If there is an obsolete and unattractive fireplace you will probably want to remove it, but do guard against taking out an original fireplace that is in keeping with the style of the house, and which could perhaps be worth a lot more than the fireplace you are thinking of installing. For example, cast-iron surrounds have a considerable resale value. What you will probably want to remove are the ugly tiled surrounds of the Fifties and Sixties. Before starting work, have the chimney swept.

The fireplace surround is usually held to the wall by screws or nails inserted through metal lugs – one on either side inserted a few inches from the top. Some larger surrounds have more than one fixing on each side.

To locate the fixings, remove the wallpaper and cut out the plaster for about 50mm (2in) around the surround using a bolster chisel and club hammer. If nails were used for fixing, these must be levered out; if screws were used it will probably be necessary to cut off the heads with a hacksaw. Have a helper steady the surround against the wall while this is done. More than likely, it will be necessary to lever the surround away from the wall using a crowbar. When it is free from the wall, join your helper(s) and lower it slowly to the ground. Be particularly careful with old cast-iron surrounds as they can be brittle, as well as surprisingly heavy.

Usually, the surround stands on the hearth and therefore it will come forward easily. However, if the surround was fitted before the hearth, then you must remove the latter first. Raised hearths are usually bedded on mortar on the floor. Insert a crowbar beneath the hearth and lever upwards to release it from the mortar bed. If the hearth is inset level with the floor, it can be left.

REMOVING A FIREPLACE

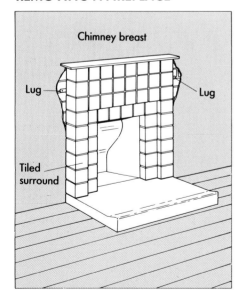

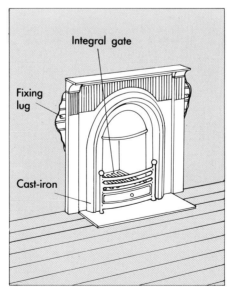

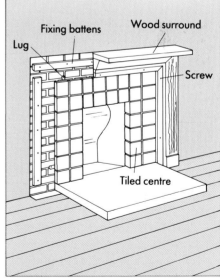

1 A tiled surround is held against the wall by fixing lugs on each side. Saw off the heads of the securing screws, then lever the surround forward and lower it to the floor. Then prise up the hearth. (If the surround rests on the floor, remove the hearth first – a crowbar should release it from the mortar bed.

2 A cast-iron fireplace, as here, has a resale value, so remove it very carefully so it can be used in another room, or sold. Again it will be held with metal lugs at each side. Cast-iron fireplaces can be heavy: you may need two people to move them. Handle them gently – they can be brittle.

3 Timber fireplace surrounds are usually fixed to battens nailed or screwed to the wall. The heads of the screws fixing the surround to the battens will be covered with filler, making them hard to locate. The tiled section will probably be held by lugs fitted to the top and sides and screwed to the brickwork.

Building a fireplace

The first step is to make sure the fireback is in place and in good condition. It is constructed in fireproof clay and comprises two separate pieces – lower half and top half – which are assembled in place to form the familiar shape within the fireplace.

If the back is cracked you should repair it, and if it is badly damaged or missing it must be replaced.

Cracks can be filled with fireclay cement while the fireback is cold. Scrape out cracks with a trowel, brush out dust, then dampen the fireback before pressing the fireclay cement into place and smoothing it.

New firebacks are made in standard sizes; measure the opening before buying a replacement. Place the lower half centrally and squarely in the opening and check that it is horizontal. Place a double layer of corrugated paper behind it, then pack behind it and the walls of the chimney with a mix comprising one part lime, two parts sand, four parts broken brick (very small pieces). Do not use cement as this will crack the fireback. If the fireplace is on an outside wall, use an insulating back-ing comprising one part cement to five parts vermiculite. Lay a small amount of fire cement on the top edge of the lower half of the fireback, then fit the top half, tapping it down into place. Again, add corrugated paper and backing behind the fireback. At the top chamfer off neatly from the knee of the fireback to the throat of the flue. Use either a cement/vermiculite mix here or a mortar mix of about one part cement to five parts sand.

If you want to build a stone fire surround, most of the manufacturers of suitable walling blocks produce

1 If necessary, fit a new fireback in the builder's opening. Pack behind the fireback with a weak insulating backing mix.

2 Lay the stones 'dry' to see how they fit together. A long stone will be required as a lintel over each of the openings.

3 Lay the stones using a suitable ready-mixed mortar, or one part cement, one part lime and four parts sand.

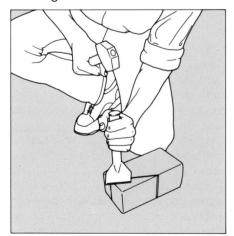

4 Some stones may have to be cut to shape: score round with a brick bolster and club hammer, then tap sharply to make the break.

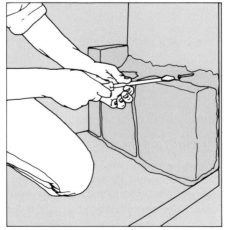

5 Long screws partially screwed in-to plastic wallplugs will tie the stonework to the main wall and keep it steady.

6 The finished fireplace. It is easy to combine a log store, TV table and video housing in a unit like this – the possibilities are endless.

designs for fireplaces which you can copy, or you can design your own fireplace or buy a fireplace kit.

Most people building a stone fireplace choose reconstructed stone because this is economical, easy to obtain, and is produced in a range of regular sizes. If you live in an area where natural local stone is widely available you may prefer to use this.

Whether you are building to your own design or with a kit, it is a good idea to lay out the stones on the ground so that the complete fireplace is created exactly as it will appear *in situ* on the wall. This gives you the opportunity to make any necessary modifications. Get any cutting of stones done as well, then build the surround as shown in the illustrations.

Brick tile fireplace

While you can build a conventional brick and stone fireplace as shown here, where the fireplace is to be purely for decoration, or for a gas or electric fire, it is a lot easier to build the surround using stick-on brick or stone tiles. These are easy to fix and give a very authentic appearance if correctly fitted in the style of genuine brick or stone. The secret of a good job is to get the bonding correct at the corners, which is easier with brick tiles rather than stone tiles because special brick corner tiles are available for external corners.

You may wonder why there is a need for brick tiles when it would be easier just to knock the plaster off the walls. The reason is that the brickwork under the plaster is very unlikely to be built of facing-quality bricks, if it is built of bricks at all! It is just as likely that the inside wall is built of walling blocks and you would not want to expose these.

Brick slips are available in a wide range of types. Some are genuine brickettes, made in a variety of brick colours from kiln-fired clay. Some types are made from gypsum plasters and these have a solid feel, but are usually only surface-coloured, a point to remember if they are to be

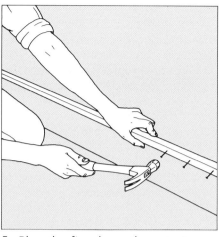

1 Plan the fireplace, then start construction by fixing a horizontal batten as a guide for the bottom course.

2 Lay the brick tiles out on the floor to achieve a balanced distribution of colours and tones.

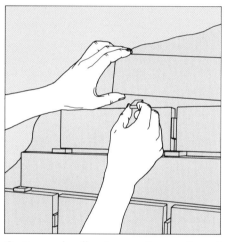

3 Spread adhesive on the wall and press the tiles into it with polystyrene spacers to separate them.

4 A very realistic brickwork effect can be achieved using brick tiles, as shown here.

fitted where they may be brushed against. Another type has a synthetic backing into which particles of a brick-like aggregate are pressed. This type can be bent or curved if required, after gentle heating.

Choosing the tiles

When planning the fireplace, try to create an effect that will be as natural as possible. Traditionally, red bricks are the most common type for building fireplaces and chimneys in the home. If you intend to cover a large area, a dark brick finish may look overpowering, so it may be more appropriate to use a lighter shade of finish.

The tiles are stuck on the wall rather like ceramic tiles, except that they must be bonded in a conventional brickwork fashion. There are many types of brickwork bonds that you can recreate.

Start by fixing a horizontal batten to the wall as a guide for the bottom course of slips. Spread the recommended adhesive on the wall, then press the slips into the adhesive using plastic spacers to keep the horizontal and vertical joints uniform. The adhesive is usually coloured to resemble mortar, so the joints can be left as they are, or the brick tiles can be pointed using pointing mortar.

Timber surround

There are now several timber surround kits on the market for those who are unable to pick up a genuine old surround.

If you find an old timber surround, after cleaning it up you can fit it around the fire opening over a subframe of battens screwed to the wall.

In the case of the hearth, the requirements are exactly the same as for any other type of fire surround – a sound concrete constructional hearth is essential. There will almost certainly be one present if you are fitting a new fireplace into an existing opening, but if you are building a new sectional flue it will be necessary to provide a concrete slab foundation that will take the weight of the chimney, fireplace and fire appliance, and provide a non-combustible area reaching out into the room.

This constructional hearth must be at least 125mm (5in) thick and must extend at least 500mm (20in) into the room and 150mm (6in) beyond each side of the builder's opening. This hearth should be topped by a superimposed hearth which is mainly decorative but must be at least 47mm (1⅞in) thick and extend at least 300mm (12in) in front of an open fire or room heater.

If the hearth is in good condition, move on to check the fireback; see page 54.

After removing an old fireplace, you will probably be left with a very rough area of wall and it will be necessary to render this area so it is smooth enough to take the infill tiles or stone slabs, or you will have to cast a fire surround back panel in concrete reinforced with several 6mm (¼in) diameter steel rods. The mould can be made from strips of plywood. If you need a new hearth, this is cast in a similar way, but in this case it is cast in position.

Whether you are fixing a conventional timber surround or a clip-together kit, the first stage is to fit a sub-frame of wall battens measuring about 50 × 50mm (2 × 2in) around the opening.

1 The original fireplace before work commenced – an early Sixties' design.

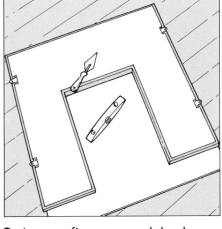

2 A new fire surround back, reinforced with steel rods, is cast in concrete.

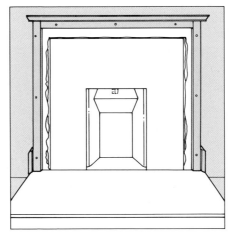

6 The completed framing around the opening. The mantelshelf must be level.

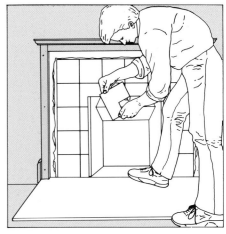

7 Reproduction Victorian tiles are fixed symmetrically over the concrete back panel.

9 The moulded boards are placed against the wall battens and screwed to them.

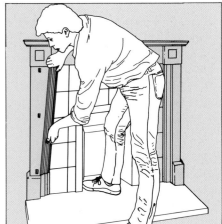

10 Using the Burbridge clip system, fix cover mouldings to the boards each side of the opening.

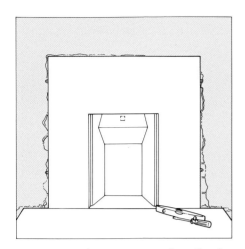

3 Mirror plates are used to fix the surround vertically in front of the fire opening.

4 This fire surround is a Burbridge kit. A wall batten is fixed to the mantelshelf underside.

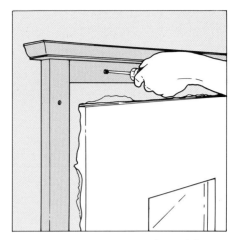

5 The mantelshelf assembly is screwed and plugged to the wall between side battens.

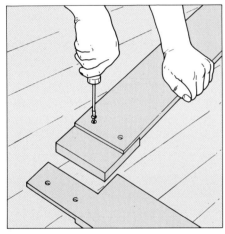

8 Working from the rear, the moulded fire surround boards are screwed to the corner blocks.

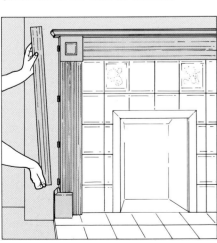

11 Glue and clip side mouldings in place on to the wall battens, resting on the base blocks.

12 The finished Burbridge fire surround after staining and varnishing.

BREAKFAST BARS

Breakfast bars are both time and space savers. They are ideal for hurried meals in a busy family and they make the most use of valuable space in a small kitchen. Properly positioned, a breakfast bar is ideal for serving from as well as for eating at and is the ideal alternative to a full kitchen table.

The height for the bar depends on the seating arrangements; for bar stools a bar height of 960mm (38in) will be suitable, while for ordinary kitchen chairs the bar should be at the usual table height of about 710mm (28in). The minimum depth for a breakfast bar should be about 460mm (18in) and there should be a knee space of at least 250mm (10in) underneath.

The bar must be sturdy and it should have a wipe-clean surface such as melamine or ceramic tiles.

There are various ways of building a breakfast bar and a great deal will depend on the style of the kitchen. A U-shaped kitchen provides a ready-made means of building a breakfast bar because the back of the peninsular units can be used to form the bar. You just need to ensure that the worktop overhangs the back of the units sufficiently for users to be able to get their knees under the bar.

Another way to build a breakfast bar is as part of a kitchen island unit and again it is necessary only to build out the unit worktop to form an overhang on one or two sides to create the bar.

With either of these two methods you can hinge the bar against the units so it folds flat when not in use, thus saving space. In this case make the bar from chipboard covered with a plastic laminate and use folding table hinges to fix the bar to the top edge of the kitchen units. On a long bar place hinges at 1200mm (4ft) intervals and fit 12 × 38mm (½ × 1½in) hardwood lipping along the front edge of the bar to prevent the bar from flexing in use.

In many cases it will be best to make a breakfast bar by building out from a suitable wall or other fixed surface. This will necessitate making the bar from a worktop fixed at one end to a batten screwed horizontally to the wall and, at the other end, given some form of support, such as timber legs, metal legs, or a low timber-framed hollow partition wall which can be covered with plasterboard, tiles, or timber cladding.

Ready-made laminated chipboard postformed worktops make excellent breakfast bars, or you may prefer to make the top from a timber frame-work covered in chipboard and then finished with ceramic tiles. In this case adjust the thickness and width of the framework to suit the size of the tiles you are using so that cutting of tiles is minimized.

It is a good idea to build drawers into the space under the breakfast bar, thereby increasing its storage capabilities. The easiest way to make the drawers is to use a proprietary drawer-making system. These usually comprise plastic drawer side, back, and front panels which clip together around a hardboard base panel. Hide the front of the drawer with a 'planted' wooden drawer front. The drawer slides on plastic runners fixed to the sides of the carcass of the bar, as shown in the illustration.

460 mm

710 mm

960 mm

Eating in comfort   250 mm

U-shaped style kitchen

Breakfast bar unit   Peninsular unit

Island unit kitchen

Breakfast bar built with mixed sizes of stone walling blocks

Breakfast bar

Kitchen island unit

Above: ideas for breakfast bars showing various ways of making use of kitchen units. The inset shows dimensions to remember when designing.

Right: the drawings show (top) a simple breakfast bar made from a timber frame covered with chipboard which is tiled, and with a plywood-covered end support; (centre) various ideas for fixing, all of which can support the weight of someone leaning on the bar; (bottom) a design with dimensions for a small bar with two-drawer storage space built in beneath.

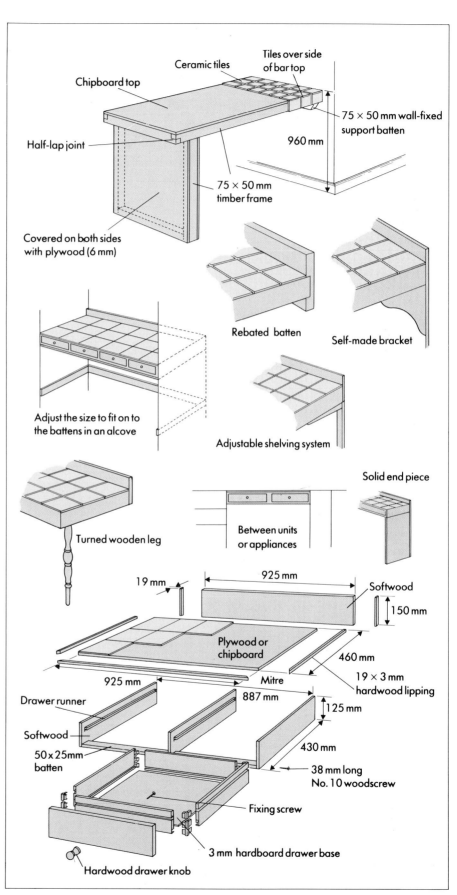

Ceramic tiles

Tiles over side of bar top

Chipboard top

75 × 50 mm wall-fixed support batten

960 mm

Half-lap joint

Covered on both sides with plywood (6 mm)

75 × 50 mm timber frame

Rebated batten

Self-made bracket

Adjust the size to fit on to the battens in an alcove

Adjustable shelving system

Turned wooden leg

Between units or appliances

Solid end piece

19 mm

925 mm

Softwood

150 mm

Plywood or chipboard

460 mm

19 × 3 mm hardwood lipping

925 mm

Mitre

887 mm

125 mm

Drawer runner

Softwood

50 x 25mm batten

430 mm

38 mm long No. 10 woodscrew

Fixing screw

3 mm hardboard drawer base

Hardwood drawer knob

Above: well planned breakfast bars can make good use of limited spaces in many kinds of kitchen.

SHOWERS

When you are considering installing a shower there are two decisions to make – which type of shower you want and where you should put it.

Fitting a shower over the bath combined with the bath taps is by far the easiest and cheapest of all the options – it gives you the extra bonus of a hand-held spray you can use for washing hair while in the bath, and it also makes cleaning out the bath a lot easier. However, it does not increase washing facilities and, in general, it is better to install a separate shower – either elsewhere in the bathroom or in another room in the house. How difficult and expensive this will be depends on the type of shower and the type of enclosure you choose, and what is involved in running water to the shower and a waste pipe away from it.

One of the most effective ways is to build a tiled shower enclosure as shown over the page. You can enclose it with a curtain or, for a deluxe shower, you can fit a purpose-made shower door.

Types of shower

Leaving aside the simple type of shower which pushes on to bath or basin taps, there are four main types of shower.

Bath/shower mixers replace the existing bath taps. No extra plumbing is required and they are nearly always designed to fit standard tap holes 182mm (7in) apart. A knob or lever on the mixer tap sends water either to the shower head or to the spout feeding the bath, and the shower head itself can be mounted on a bracket or a slider rail.

Shower mixer valves have their own plumbing supplies from the hot and cold water and can be positioned either over the bath or in a separate enclosure or cubicle. Both thermostatic and nonthermostatic (cheaper) versions are available. There is

Above and left: purpose-built showers make effective use of corner spaces in these bathrooms.

usually a choice of having a surface-mounted valve, where the plumbing pipes are exposed, or a flush-fitted valve where they are all concealed. The latter is usually more expensive and is more difficult to fit.

Power showers are the latest type and are different from normal shower valves in that a twin-impeller pump (or two pumps) is located in both the hot and cold supply to the shower valve. Because the water is under pressure, the shower delivers much more of it (three or more times as much) and there is a choice of spray patterns, usually including a 'needle' spray and an aerated 'champagne' spray.

A power shower could be fitted over the bath (with appropriate screening) but normally requires its own separate enclosure or cubicle.

Instantaneous electric showers are connected to the rising cold water main, but even so do not give very high flow rates. They need their own electric circuit and some modern electric showers have ratings of 8kW or more (often with a lower summer setting). Remote-control types are available where only a control panel is positioned in the showering area (over the bath or in a separate enclosure or cubicle) with the main heater elsewhere.

Where to put it

All types of shower can be put over a bath, but you will generally need a shower curtain or shower screen to prevent water splashing on the floor. This will add to the cost, and you may also need to add tiling further up the wall next to the bath.

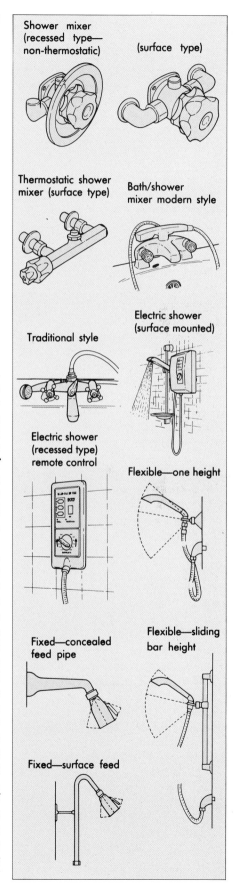

Left: purpose-built shower enclosure with inward-folding door.
Right: a selection of generally available shower mixers and heads.

Shower mixer (recessed type—non-thermostatic)

(surface type)

Thermostatic shower mixer (surface type)

Bath/shower mixer modern style

Traditional style

Electric shower (surface mounted)

Electric shower (recessed type) remote control

Flexible—one height

Fixed—concealed feed pipe

Flexible—sliding bar height

Fixed—surface feed

The problem with baths is that they are designed for sitting in rather than standing up in. It is much better to have a purpose-made shower enclosure or cubicle with a flat-bottomed tray.

The size of shower tray varies from 750 to 800mm (29½ to 31½in) square and, when considering where to put it, remember to leave at least this amount of space in front of it as well.

You can build a separate enclosure on to a shower tray by using a combination of existing walls, new stud partition walls, shower side screens and doors or curtains. Building a shower into a corner is often a good choice as you can use two existing walls – special corner doors are available and you can even get curved corner shower trays. The problem with building a separate shower enclosure is the cost – not just of the side screens and the doors but also of tiling any existing walls.

To cut down on the amount of work, you can install a freestanding shower cubicle which has the advantage that most of the plumbing pipes will be concealed. Some cubicles come already fitted with shower valves or instantaneous electric showers and only need connecting.

Plumbing-in

The first consideration with the plumbing is the type of water supply you have in your house. If it is direct, where all the cold taps and toilets in the house are fed directly from the mains, the only type of shower you can usually fit is an electric type. If the cold supply comes from the storage cistern and the hot from a hot water cylinder, you can choose any type.

From a plumbing point of view, the bath/shower mixer is by far the easiest to fit as it simply replaces the existing bath taps. The only problem you are likely to have is where the old pipes do not meet the new tap tails (a problem which can be solved by using hand-bendable copper pipe or flexible plastic pipe for the final connection), or where the tap holes in the bath are the wrong distance apart. This is likely to happen only on very old baths, but there are some Victorian-type bath/shower mixers with swivelling tap tails which can accommodate different spacings. One other problem with a bath/shower mixer is that it can run scalding hot if the basin cold tap is run, or the toilet flushed, at the same time as the shower is being used, starving it of water.

CONSTRUCTION OF SHOWER ENCLOSURE

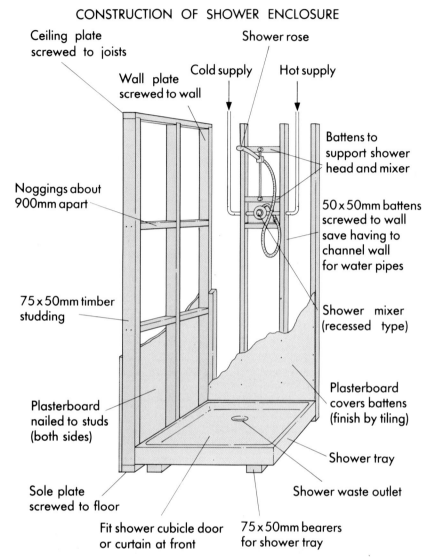

Ceiling plate screwed to joists

Shower rose

Wall plate screwed to wall

Cold supply   Hot supply

Battens to support shower head and mixer

50 x 50mm battens screwed to wall save having to channel wall for water pipes

Noggings about 900mm apart

75 x 50mm timber studding

Shower mixer (recessed type)

Plasterboard covers battens (finish by tiling)

Plasterboard nailed to studs (both sides)

Shower tray

Shower waste outlet

Sole plate screwed to floor

Fit shower cubicle door or curtain at front

75 x 50mm bearers for shower tray

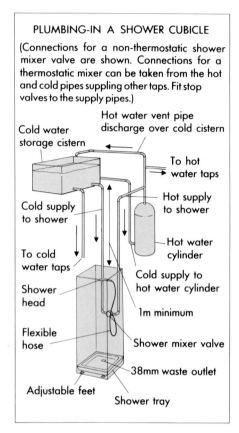

PLUMBING-IN A SHOWER CUBICLE

(Connections for a non-thermostatic shower mixer valve are shown. Connections for a thermostatic mixer can be taken from the hot and cold pipes suppling other taps. Fit stop valves to the supply pipes.)

Cold water storage cistern

Hot water vent pipe discharge over cold cistern

To hot water taps

Cold supply to shower

Hot supply to shower

To cold water taps

Hot water cylinder

Shower head

Cold supply to hot water cylinder

Flexible hose

1m minimum

Shower mixer valve

38mm waste outlet

Adjustable feet

Shower tray

Shower mixer valves can suffer from this problem as well, but there are two ways of combating it. The first is to run a new 15mm (½in) cold supply pipe from the cold water cistern just to the shower: the second is to fit a thermostatic type of shower which will compensate for the drop in pressure. If you choose a thermostatic type, you can connect both hot and cold supply pipes into the supply in the bathroom, or take them from the pipes leading from the cold water cistern and hot water cylinder. For up to 5m (16½ft) of pipe run, 15mm (½in) pipes are suitable; for runs of over 5m (16½ft), use 22mm (¾in) pipes.

A further problem with both bath/ shower mixers and shower mixer valves is the available pressure head. This is measured as the distance from the shower rose to the bottom of the cold water cistern, and if it is less than around one metre (39in) you are unlikely to get a proper shower.

You can increase the head by raising the cold water cistern in the loft on to an elevated platform, but this increases the risk of frozen or burst pipes. The other alternative is to fit a shower pump, but this will add considerably to the cost of the shower.

The plumbing connections to a power shower are more complicated than for a shower mixer valve. The cold supply must come as a new pipe from the cold water cistern, and with the majority of showers, the hot supply needs to come via an Essex

flange connected to the side of the hot water cylinder, rather than as a connection from the open vent pipe at the top of the cylinder. The reason for this is the amount of water the shower uses – this could suck out the contents of the open vent pipe. Both pipes will need to be 22mm (¾in) but there is no worry about pressure head – many pumped and power showers can be fitted with the shower rose above the cold water cistern, which makes these types very suitable for showers in loft conversions.

An instantaneous electric shower needs only a connection to the rising main. Downstairs, this can be tee-jointed in near the kitchen sink; upstairs it will often be easier to join it in the loft space, with the supply pipe to the shower (fitted with an isolating stop valve) brought down through the ceiling.

Plumbing-out

Showers installed over a bath do not create a problem for running the waste pipe – the existing bath waste will take the dirty water away.

Showers installed elsewhere in separate enclosures or cubicles will need a waste pipe run to the main soil stack (for single-stack waste systems), or to the upstairs hopper head (or downstairs gully) for two-pipe waste systems. The size of waste pipe needed is 38mm (1½in) up to a distance of 3m (10ft) and 50mm (2in) for lengths up to 4m (13ft).

For connecting to a plastic soil stack, you will need a strap-on or self-locking connector boss unless there is a spare boss on the stack. Lay the pipe with a minimum fall of 19mm (¾in) in every metre run – maximum 90mm/metre (3½in/39in) – to which you must add the depth of the necessary trap fitted beneath the shower tray. To make life easier, you can mount the shower tray on a plinth, with a removable front for access to the trap in case it gets blocked. It will not usually be possible to fit a deep-seal (75mm/3in) trap as required by the Building Regulations for single-stack plumbing, however, and you will have to use a shallow-seal (38 or 50mm/1½ or 2in) one instead. Even so, it will generally be possible to run the waste pipe only between, and parallel with, flooring joists rather than across them, unless, that is, the waste can be taken straight out through the wall above floor level.

Electric supply

An electric instantaneous shower needs its own electricity supply run from the consumer unit. This must be fused at 30 amps for showers up to 9.6kW, and the size of cable needed is a minimum of $6mm^2$. If there is no spare way on the consumer unit, you will need to install a separate switched fuse unit near to the consumer unit. This has to be connected to the meter (by the Electricity Board) with $16mm^2$ single-core cables.

A 30 (or 45) amp double-pole switch must be installed close to the shower. It must be the ceiling-mounted pullcord type if accessible from the bath or shower cubicle.

Tiling

It is essential to use waterproof tile adhesive when fixing ceramic tiles in a shower cubicle. Before tiling, inject a bead of clear silicone rubber sealant into the joint between the shower tray and the wall as a second line of defence.

Careful setting out is vital, with the tiles centralized on the walls, and whole tiles at the top where they are most likely to be seen. Keep cut tiles close to the shower tray.

Support the tiles on a horizontal batten while the adhesive sets. Finish by grouting joints with *waterproof* grout and seal around the tray with silicone sealant.

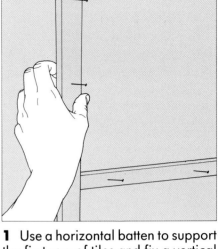

1 Use a horizontal batten to support the first row of tiles and fix a vertical batten at the starting point.

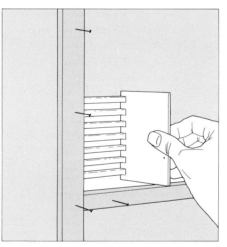

2 Use waterproof tiling adhesive and apply it with the spreader provided to cover about 1 sq m/yd.

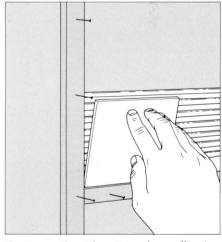

3 Press the tiles into the adhesive with a slight twist. Use plastic spacers if the tiles do not have lugs.

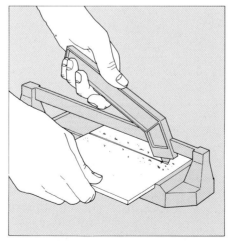

4 A tile scoring and cutting tool like this is not expensive and is a boon if there are many tiles to cut.

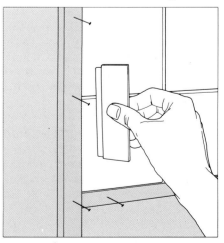

5 Apply waterproof grout with a rubber blade squeegee; wipe off surplus; polish the tiles next day.

LOFTS

Most people are short of space in the home and while their first reaction may be to think of moving or building an extension, a better alternative may be to convert the loft space. If you want to convert a loft to an extra bedroom or other habitable room you will need to call in a builder and have plans drawn up and officially approved.

On the other hand, the answer could be to convert the loft area for storage, or as a hobbies room, and in this case there is a lot you can do for yourself. By moving things into the loft you will create extra space elsewhere in the house, and this could be just sufficient to provide the extra accommodation required without going to the expense of moving.

To get safe access into the loft it is easy to install a loft ladder, and many foldaway designs now feature twin handrails for safety.

To make the area useful for storage you will require good lighting and flat flooring that is easy to walk on, although before you lay it you may need to strengthen the floor with additional joists.

Finally, there will be insulation to attend to and perhaps the building of partition walls.

Start by looking at the loft to see whether it is suitable even for storage, let alone additional living space. If there is a loft hatch, use a tall pair of steps with a handrail to get into the loft. Will this hatchway be large enough to allow you to get suitcases and perhaps larger items into the loft? If necessary you can enlarge a hatchway. At the same time it would be sensible to fit a proper fold-away loft ladder to make it easy, and safe, to get into the loft whenever necessary.

If there is no hatchway, making one is a DIY job you can carry out. The method is as for enlarging a loft hatchway (see pages 68/69), although first you will have to pull down an area of ceiling (which is a very messy job) so that you can see into the loft.

Once you are in the loft you can decide if it is suitable for storage, and perhaps for hobby use. If there are struts and purlins you may be able to work round them when moving trunks, cases, discarded furniture, and other bric-a-brac into the loft. If you need to move struts and other roof supports out of the way, do not do so without first consulting a reputable builder. Generally speaking, older traditional-type loft spaces are quite easy to convert for extra storage space, while modern low-pitched roofs with trussed rafters are not suitable for conversion. You also need to ascertain whether there is enough headroom in the loft area (2.3m headroom over

a major part of the area is the height to aim for, although there are no hard and fast rules when the loft is being used for storage and hobbies).

One way to get height into a loft room is to install dormer windows, which is definitely not a DIY job. However, to get light into a loft it is feasible to install a roof window and

Is your loft suitable for conversion to a storage area or hobbies room?

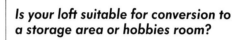

1 A typical modern trussed-rafter roof. The rafters and struts are held together with metal plates. The struts cannot be moved and all you can do in this case is partly floor the loft and store lightweight items between the struts.

2 A trussed purlin roof. In this case there is plenty of room between the purlins and you can floor the central area and use it for storage or hobbies.

3 A traditional roof with strutted purlins. This loft space can be converted, but get a builder to fit new supports for the purlins before struts are removed.

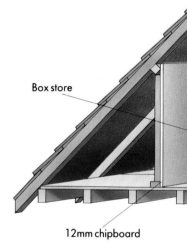

9.5mm plasterboard

Box store

12mm chipboard

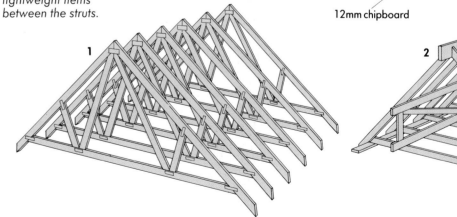

1

2

one or more of these can make all the difference to how a loft is used. Modern roof windows are double glazed, they are easy to install from inside the roof space, and they are reversible, which allows them to be cleaned from the inside. They are also fully weatherstripped. A roof window will also allow you to ventilate the loft area, which is vital if you are going to use it as a hobbies room.

If you are careful in the height you choose to install a roof window you can often obtain a very good view from the loft room. However, the sill of a roof window should not be too low or there could be a danger of children falling out.

An opening roof window makes an excellent means of escape in the event of a fire. To this end a roof window should be at least 850mm (33in) high and 500mm (20in) wide when open, with the bottom of the opening not more than 1.1m (43in) above floor level.

Bungalow roof conversions are usually easier than house loft conversions. They are often larger than the roofs of houses offering similar accommodation, and usually more accessible.

Features such as the water system and chimneys may force you to make your conversion at one end of the loft. There is not a lot you can do about chimneys, but water tanks and pipework are usually quite easy to move thanks to easy-to-plumb modern fittings.

Electrical work is also something you can do yourself. As long as you feel competent with wiring and switch off at the mains, it should be straightforward to put in lighting points and power outlets if these are required. If you want heating in the loft, electric heating is usually the easiest to install.

Even if you are only using the loft for storage, insulation is a must. If the roof is not lined (if you can see the battens and backs of the tiles or slates from inside the loft space), line the rafters with waterproof building paper. This will stop draughts and prevent rain and snow being blown on to the articles you will be storing in the loft. It will also help to keep them free of dust. Work from the apex of the roof, and pin the building paper horizontally to the undersides of the rafters, overlapping adjacent sheets and finishing by tucking the building paper into the eaves.

Insulating the floor

A loft room that is to be used as a living room will not need floor insulation – it makes sense to allow the heat from the rooms below to rise up through the loft room floor. Here you would be paying special attention to lining the roof itself to prevent heat escaping.

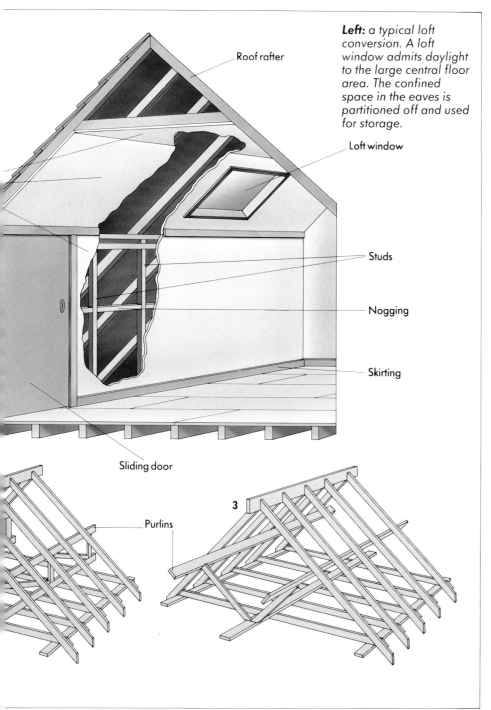

Roof rafter

Left: a typical loft conversion. A loft window admits daylight to the large central floor area. The confined space in the eaves is partitioned off and used for storage.

Loft window

Studs

Nogging

Skirting

Sliding door

Purlins

3

However, a loft that is to be used purely for storage, or as an occasional workroom or hobbies room, does need floor insulation. The simplest and quickest way to insulate is to use glassfibre blanket which is sold in rolls. This is just wide enough to fit between standard joist widths with a little extra to spare. Since it can cause skin irritation, protective gloves and long sleeves are sensible precautions to use when handling it.

You start to lay a roll at the eaves. Use a pole to push the tail of the roll well down into the eaves. Do not block the airflow completely though, or condensation may become a problem. Unroll the glassfibre between the joists until you reach roughly the centre of the loft. Cut the roll there. Go to the other end of the loft and repeat the procedure. When you get to the middle of the loft, cut the end of the roll to meet the other end.

Bring electric cables on top of the insulation. Where it crosses a joist cut a shallow notch and cover the cable with a steel plate. Plumbing pipe work can remain below the blanket where it will be well protected from freeze-ups.

You will need to insulate the cold water tank and central heating feed tank. This can be done with glassfibre blanket, or 25mm (1in) thick polystyrene slabs. It is best not to insulate the floor below the tank since any heat rising from below will help prevent freeze-ups. However, it is essential to cover the top so that dirt, spiders and so on cannot fall into the water. Protect any exposed pipework by wrapping it in purpose-made pipewrap.

WALLS

If you really want to get the best from your loft storage/hobby room it is well worthwhile lining the walls with plasterboard. You simply nail the plasterboard to a timber framework called a stud partition. You will find it easier to build the partition on the floor of the loft and then lift it into place and fix it to the rafters and floor by nailing.

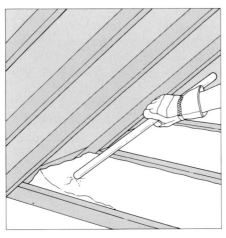

1 Insulate the loft floor with glassfibre blanket. Tuck this into the eaves if the roof is unlined, but do not block any ventilation holes.

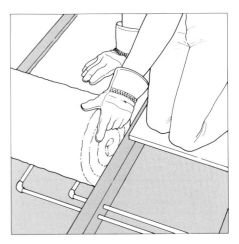

2 Lay the insulation over water pipes, but bring electric cables to the surface if possible, to make them easy to find.

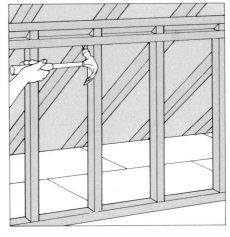

5 Assemble the wall frame on the floor of the loft and then fix it in place under the roof purlin or rafters using wedges and long nails.

6 To form an access opening, cut out the soleplate and part of a stud and fit a nogging across. Line the opening with planed timber.

The framework consists of a timber sole plate fixed to the floor, a head plate nailed to the rafters (or to a roof purlin if there is one of these at the wall position) with vertical timbers between them, called studs, which give this type of partition its name. Cut the head plate, sole plate, and studs from 75 × 50mm (3 × 2in) sawn timber. Nail the studs between the head and sole plate at 400mm (16in) intervals. If the walls are up to 1m (39in) high there will be no need for noggings (horizontal timbers) between the studs, but walls over 1m will need them. Cut the noggings from 75 × 38mm (3 × 1½in) sawn timber.

To give access to the void behind a loft wall, form an access hatch in the partition wall. Leave out a stud and fix a nogging between the two studs that are left. Nail a short length of stud between the head plate and the nogging at the top of the opening. You can nail battens around the opening to line it and to give a fixing for an access hatch.

To fit the partition wall frame, wedge it in place between the floor and the underside of a purlin or the underside of the rafters. Check that

3 Make sure the cold water storage cistern is well wrapped, with a funnel to catch feed and expansion water. Do not insulate under cistern.

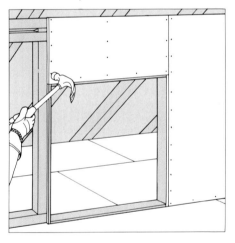

4 Tongued and grooved chipboard panels are ideal for flooring. End joins should be staggered and co-incide with joists.

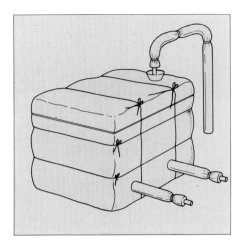

7 Fit insulation between the studs. Foil-backed glassfibre blanket is stapled to the studs; other types can be supported from behind with netting.

8 Nail the plasterboard in place with the vapour check membrane or foil against the timber stud wall framework.

the frame is vertical. Cut triangular blocks to fit the gaps between the top of the head plate and the underside of the purlin or rafters. Fix the frame by nailing into the rafters or purlin, and into the floor joists, through the flooring boards.

It will be best to fit wall insulation between the studs before fixing the plasterboard in place. The easiest to fit is called 'flanged' foil-backed insulation which is like a conventional glassfibre blanket bonded to tough foil-backed paper. The paper has 'ears' which enable you to staple it to the studs with the foil side facing the

room and the insulation facing the void. This vapour check will stop moisture from the room getting to the roof timbers. Alternatively, fit plasterboard with a built-in vapour barrier.

Nail the plasterboard in place with galvanized plasterboard nails at 150mm (6in) intervals and finish the joints with jointing tape and joint filler.

FLOORS

Unless you want to use the loft only for storage of lightweight items you

will have to strengthen the floor before laying sheets of flooring over the existing joists. These are often not very large and certainly not substantial enough to take the weight of heavy loads and people walking in the loft.

One way to strengthen the floor is to fit extra joists of the same size as the originals, to share the load. You can lay these alongside the original joists and bolted to them, or you can fit them in between, in which case you may need to support them in metal joist hangers if the original joists are notched into a larger beam.

For a really sturdy floor fit a new full-size floor joist over a loadbearing wall at each side of the loft, then fit new floor joists 480mm (16in) apart between these joists, holding them in place with metal joist hangers.

Once you have strengthened the floor you can lay new flooring on the joists. You can use ordinary tongued and grooved floorboards, but an ideal material is tongued and grooved chipboard panels. These are cheap and easy to lay, and because they are available in manageable sizes they pass easily through the loft hatch.

Lay the floor after you have positioned any electric wiring and plumbing pipes that are needed. Be sure to leave screwed-down access panels over areas which you may need to get at for maintenance, such as over electric joint boxes. Remove the tongues from the panels at these points so they can be lifted easily.

Ceilings

The ceiling of the loft room will be the underside of the rafters, and if you are using the loft space as a hobby room you will want to board in this area and insulate it at the same time. Building paper as a lining, as mentioned previously, is only suitable when the loft is to be used for storage.

A simple way to insulate and line the ceiling in one go is to fit thermal plasterboard, which is plasterboard bonded to expanded polystyrene. You just nail or screw it to the underside of the rafters. It is available up to 50mm (2in) thick, so it could reduce headroom significantly.

An alternative is to fit slabs of expanded polystyrene or lengths of glassfibre blanket between the rafters. The insulation should be at least 50mm (2in) away from the underside of the roof to allow air to circulate, and over the surface there should be a polythene, building paper, or foil vapour barrier. Alternatively, nail up vapour-check or foil-backed plasterboard on the surface.

To avoid having to fix the lining right up to the ridge of the roof, you can make a ceiling by nailing horizontal timber beams between the rafters at about 2.3m (7½ft) above the floor.

Fitting a loft ladder

It is dangerous to climb into a loft without a proper loft ladder.

There are two main types of loft ladders – the telescopic type with sliding sections, and the concertina type which opens out like lazy tongs.

The telescopic type is most widely available. It has two or three sliding sections which retract into the loft space; the more sections it has the less space it takes up in the loft. This type of ladder may have one or two handrails, which are ideal for safety; it comes in both aluminium alloy and timber. The latter is more expensive, but looks more like a traditional stairway.

Concertina ladders are made from aluminium and are generally not as sturdy as the sliding-section type. However, they rest closed up on top of the loft hatch when not in use and therefore take up very little loft space.

Before buying a loft ladder, measure the height from the loft floor to the landing floor, the clearance above the loft hatch, and the dimensions of the loft hatchway. This will enable you to choose a suitable loft ladder. You may need to enlarge the hatchway, but this is

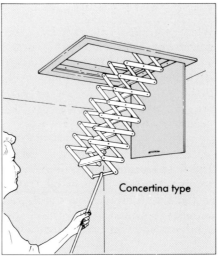

A concertina-type loft ladder

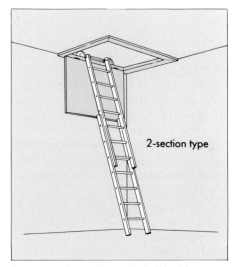

A two-section telescopic loft ladder

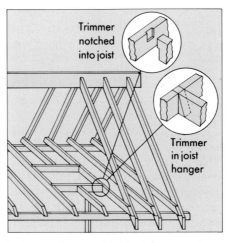

1 To enlarge the hatch opening, prop up the joist while you cut it and fit trimmer joists across the gap.

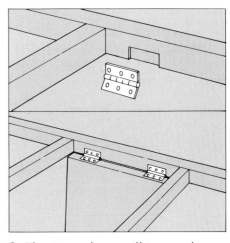

2 The trap door will open downwards. Trim it to fit inside the opening and cut recesses for the hinges.

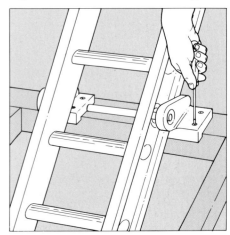

4 The ladder pivot enables the ladder to lie flat in the loft. Fit it firmly to a joist or trimmer joist.

generally not a difficult job.

The minimum size of opening required will be specified by the manufacturer. It is quite easy to enlarge an existing opening or form a completely new opening by cutting away a ceiling joist (after supporting it if necessary) and refixing the cut ends to two short lengths of joists (called trimmers) fixed between the adjacent joists. Fix the trimmers using joist hangers, or by notching them into the existing joists, or simply by nailing them in place. The ends of the cut ceiling joist should also be nailed to the trimmers. If you need to reduce the opening width, fix a short length of joist between the trimmers to one side of the opening.

Line the sides of the opening with planed timber. Cut and fit a new loft hatch from 19mm (¾in) plywood or chipboard. Fit doorstop to the lining above the hatch.

Fitting a loft stairway is straightforward following the manufacturer's instructions, which usually cover any modifications needed. In most cases this involves altering the loft hatch to hinge downwards, and fitting it with a touch-latch. Assemble the ladder and screw its pivot hinges to the loft opening. Place it at the correct angle, fit a stop, and fit the handrail. Finally, check that the ladder operates and folds correctly.

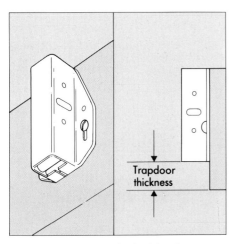

3 A special catch holds the trapdoor in place when it is closed. Fit it to allow for the thickness of the door.

5 Fit the handrail and the stop that holds the ladder at the correct angle and check that it holds firm.

TIMBER TREATMENT

When you are in the loft, either making the initial survey of work to be done, or carrying out the conversion, keep an eye open for timber problems, such as woodworm attacks, wet rot, and dry rot. All need treatment before other work.

Woodworm

The first sign of trouble is likely to be small holes in the wood rafters and joists together with small piles of dust produced by wood-destroying beetles. The larvae (woodworms)

progressively tunnel through the wood feeding on it and growing.

Eradication of woodworm is achieved by chemical treatment with a suitable preservative insecticide, sold as woodworm fluid. Apply it to the timber over all clean, bare wood surfaces, and particularly to end-grain, joints, cracks and crevices. The fluid soaks down through the wood, killing the larvae and protecting the wood against future attack for years to come.

Of course, this chemical treatment does not replace the strength of any timber that has been eaten away. If the wood is structurally unsound then you will need to replace it with new wood that has been treated with preservative to prevent it from succumbing to the same fate.

When spraying, use a garden-type, coarse, non-atomising spray with relatively low pressure to minimize splash back. Avoid breathing in the fumes and wear synthetic rubber gloves and eye protection. Use a face mask and keep ventilation as high as possible.

Further precautionary advice is given on every container of fluid. It should always be consulted.

Wood decay

There are several species of fungi responsible for wood decay in and around buildings, including loft spaces. However, dry rot is different from the rest which are called wet rot. The dry rot fungus can spread from the initial damp wood to other drier areas in order to destroy any wood it finds in its path. The wet rot fungi are confined to the wet area and do not spread beyond it.

Wet rot   *Dry rot*

It is important, when you discover an outbreak of decay, to be certain which type of rot it is, since this affects the treatment and the extent of the work that will follow.

New growth of dry rot is white and fluffy and it produces thick root-like strands.

The fungus breaks down the wood so that it losses its strength and shape, changes colour and cracks both with and across the grain.

Since wet rot is caused by more than one organism, there is no particular set of features to identify it, but cracks across the grain are rare.

If you find rot in the roof space, call in a special timber preservation company to ascertain the extent of the problem. If wet rot is the cause you may be able to make repairs yourself, but make sure that the new timber and surrounding wood is thoroughly soaked in preservative.

Apart from slipped and missing slates and tiles, one of the commonest causes of damp is lack of ventilation in the roof space which results in condensation, damp timbers and decay. Therefore ensure that there is good ventilation in the loft space by leaving air gaps at the eaves and spaces between tiling battens and any ceiling insulation you may have installed.

PERGOLAS

A pergola is an excellent decorative feature for a garden – just the place to grow flowering climbers and ideal for giving a shady retreat on those summer days when it is just too hot to sit in the sun.

Basically a pergola is a series of linked arches, usually made of timber, which can follow a straight line, be rectangular (over a patio, for example), or even turn a corner or two to make a pleasant walkway. The options are as varied as are the materials and construction methods with which you can work. A freestanding pergola on timber pillars is very uncomplicated, or one side of a pergola can be built on to the house. Yet another option is to build the structure on substantial brick or stone piers. Most people opt for either a sawn timber or rustic pole pergola.

Timber pergola

The most popular pergola is an all-timber construction using sawn timber or rustic poles. If you use sawn timber, there is a wider range of wood from which to choose. The best softwood is the naturally rot-resistant western red cedar. However, other softwoods, such as red deal, douglas fir and hemlock, can be used. Ideally, the timber will have been pressure-treated with wood preservative by your supplier, otherwise you should soak it in preservative before use – you can dig a trench in the garden and line it with thick polythene to make a soaking trough for preservative. If you are going to train climbers on the pergola, use a preservative that is harmless to plants. If you are making a rustic pergola, chestnut poles are best for rot resistance, although pine poles are more readily available. Again, both types should be soaked in wood preservative. With both sawn timber and rustic poles, remember to re-treat the exposed timber after cutting joints.

When designing a pergola you should make sure that it is about 2.4m (8ft) high which will allow adequate headroom under it once it is covered in plants. You must also allow adequate width so that you will not be scratched when walking underneath it. As a rule, a pergola should be 600mm (2ft) wider on each side than the path to allow plenty of room for straggling (and sometimes prickly) climbers.

If you are using sawn timber, a suitable size for the uprights is 75 × 75 mm (3 × 3in) and this allows you to use hammer-in steel fence-post supports to hold the uprights. Space the posts about 1.5m (5ft) apart and bolt them at the top to 150 × 50mm (6 × 2in) main bearers. If you are building the pergola against a house wall on one side, use expanding bolts to fix a 100 × 50mm (4 × 2in) wallplate to the house wall at a suitable height.

Fit 100 × 50mm (4 × 2in) timber cross beams between the main bearers, or between the main bearer and

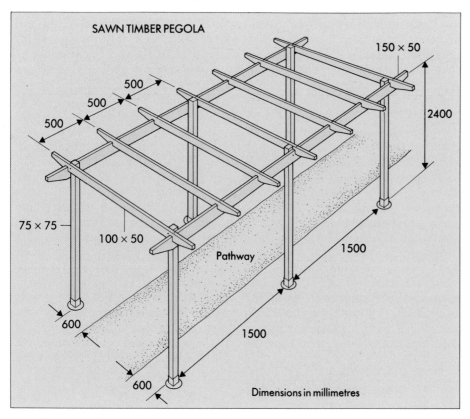

SAWN TIMBER PEGOLA

150 × 50

500
500
500
500

2400

75 × 75

100 × 50

Pathway

1500

1500

600

600

Dimensions in millimetres

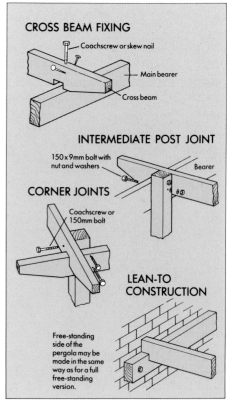

CROSS BEAM FIXING

Coachscrew or skew nail

Main bearer

Cross beam

INTERMEDIATE POST JOINT

150 x 9mm bolt with nut and washers

Bearer

CORNER JOINTS

Coachscrew or 150mm bolt

LEAN-TO CONSTRUCTION

Free-standing side of the pergola may be made in the same way as for a full free-standing version.

the wall plate. Notch and nail them to the main bearer, or fix them to it using angle brackets or metal straps. The cross beams should be long enough to protrude across the main bearers, and the ends of the cross beams can be shaped for an attractive appearance.

If you want additional shade or privacy under a pergola, fit trellis panels between the uprights.

Rustic pergola

A rustic pergola is fairly easy to make because precise joints are not necessary; you will be relying on large galvanized nails for a sound fixing. Suitable poles will range from 50 to 125mm (2 to 5in) in diameter. Use the larger poles for the uprights and main bearers and the smaller poles can be the cross beams. You can peel the poles or leave the bark on, although be prepared for this to fall off in time, a process that can give the structure a rather untidy appearance.

The joints for making a pergola are quite easy to form. Join the poles crosswise by overlapping and nail-ing, or bolting them together. You can make a neater finish by notch-ing the poles to make a flat butt joint between vertical and top horizontal members. Join intermediate rails to uprights using vee-joints and, to strengthen a rustic pergola, it is a good idea to fit corner braces which are notched and nailed to the up-rights and horizontal poles.

Planters

Planters not only have to survive all weather conditions, they spend their life full of wet soil. Consequently, it is important to make planters from materials that will not rot.

An excellent choice is concrete blocks and weather-resistant types of brick. You can build these round to form an enclosure with vertical gaps between bricks or blocks in the first one or two courses to act as weep holes for water to escape – it is most important that the soil in a planter should not become water-logged.

The problem with a brick or block planter is that it cannot be moved, so you may prefer a timber one. You

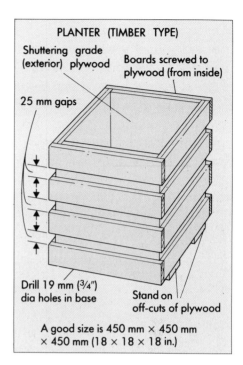

PLANTER (TIMBER TYPE)

Shuttering grade (exterior) plywood

Boards screwed to plywood (from inside)

25 mm gaps

Drill 19 mm (¾") dia holes in base

Stand on off-cuts of plywood

A good size is 450 mm × 450 mm × 450 mm (18 × 18 × 18 in.)

can make a simple planter from four pieces of shuttering grade (exterior) plywood to form a box, with another piece for the base. Screw wide boards spaced about 25mm (1in) apart to the outside of the planter for a sim-ple, effective decoration.

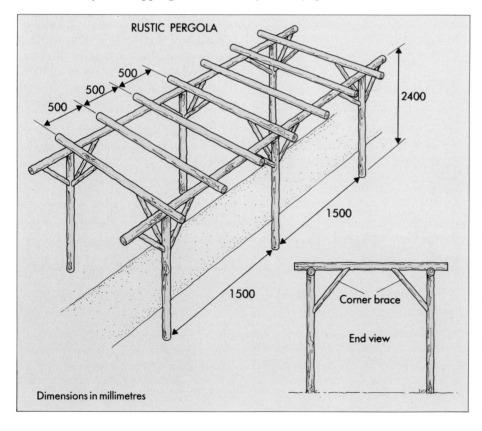

RUSTIC PERGOLA

500
500
500
2400
1500
1500

Corner brace

End view

Dimensions in millimetres

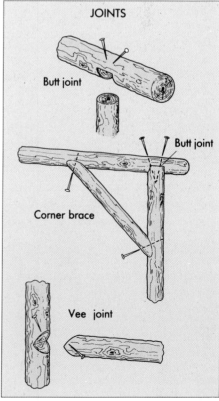

JOINTS

Butt joint

Butt joint

Corner brace

Vee joint

BARBECUES

Outdoor cooking and eating have never been so popular. That special aroma and taste, coupled with the informality and relaxation of outdoor living, have contributed to the spread of the barbecue habit. It is now a well established part of our summer lifestyle.

Barbecues come in a variety of shapes and sizes, from the simple to the sophisticated, and you can buy them ready-made or for building in. Basically, they all comprise a firebox with a grill rack above on which to cook the food. A basic barbecue uses charcoal which you have to light and discard when the meal is over; gas or electric types heat up reusable lava rocks to do the cooking.

Open-fire barbecues are the usual type for grilling; closed-fire barbecues have a lid which reflects heat downwards, browning meat all round and thus being ideal for roasts and whole joints.

Above: the look of Cotswold dry-stone walling for this elegant barbecue.

First of all you must decide what type of barbecue you need. You can make your own permanent built-in barbecue, you can build a stand for a small table-top barbecue, or you can buy a proprietary barbecue which has a stand (and perhaps wheels for mobility) to bring it up to waist height.

A proprietary barbecue is a good introduction to barbecuing. Most comprise a firebox and grill rack surrounded by a metal windshield which helps to prevent charcoal sparks from blowing about and conserves heat. The majority are fitted with legs that can be detached for storage – barbecues soon rust if left outdoors all the time. The firebox and grill on this type may be square or circular; it does not matter which, but it is important to be able to raise or lower the grill height as this is the only way of controlling the cooking speed. Most types also have

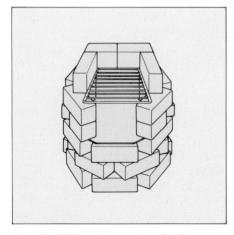

A makeshift barbecue using bricks or walling blocks with a metal oven grill and a sheet of steel for the firebed.

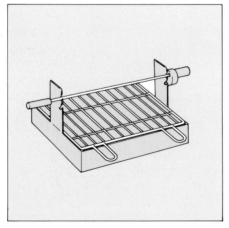

A typical barbecue kit, large and solid, for building into a purpose-made barbecue unit on a patio.

A permanent barbecue unit after the barbecue kit has been built in, with storage space underneath.

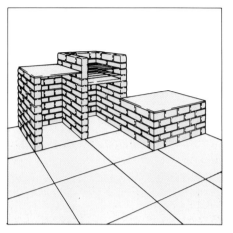

1 Following the design, lay out the first course of blocks or bricks 'dry' to check positioning.

2 Lay the blocks in mortar with a string line to ensure straight edges. Trim off any excess mortar.

3 The joints between blocks can be pointed after a couple of hours, but do not use the barbecue for a week.

notches in the edges of the windshield which serve as a housing for a spit rod. The simplest rods are turned manually, but battery-operated rods are a good idea as these ensure that spit-roasted food is evenly cooked.

Barbecues vary considerably in sophistication. The wagon types are on wheels which is useful for allowing you to wheel the barbecue into the garden for use, or under cover if it starts to rain halfway through the meal. Gas barbecues often have instant push-button lighting, easy-clean grill trays, warming racks and dual burners.

Once you have become experienced at barbecuing you may want to design and build a permanent barbecue on the patio. An ideal position is close to the house in a sheltered yet sunny position. This ensures that the kitchen is close at hand for a supply of food, crockery and utensils.

There is a fire hazard with a barbecue, so make sure yours is built away from overhanging trees, bushes and long, dry grass.

When you come to build a barbecue you will probably want to use walling blocks or bricks to match the patio or house. A selection of designs is shown here; most people have in their mind a design that will suit them best. Barbecue grills and fire-

Above: a variety of free-standing proprietary barbecues is available, including gas-burning models and mobile versions mounted on wheels.

boxes for building into permanent structures are available, and most come with suggestions for building a suitable barbecue to house them.

Key components of a permanent barbecue set-up are a housing for the barbecue firebox, of course, and a grill that is easily adjustable for height. A covered fuel store is useful, together with a slab at around grill-height which you can use for food preparation. A seat close by is also a good idea and this can double as a food serving area.

The actual dimensions for the barbecue enclosure will be given by the grill manufacturers, and they will also specify the height for the tray. A useful height for the fire tray is about 690mm (27in) and the grill tray should have built-in galvanized metal supports one, two and three courses above the fire tray. You can rest the barbecue components on the supports while the barbecue is in use, storing them under cover at other times. The walls surrounding the grill tray should be built up slightly to act as a windbreak. If you incorporate a seat, the height for this should be about 430mm (17in).

A permanent barbecue should be built on paving or a hard concrete base, but if you want just a temporary barbecue for a one-off party you can create one by simply stacking bricks around an oven grill tray.

GARDEN STEPS

Garden steps make an interesting visual feature in a garden and take you comfortably from one level to another where perhaps a lawn slopes steeply, or a patio is set well below or above the garden level. Although there are no building regulations governing the way steps are designed and constructed, there are basic, commonsense factors governing what should or should not be done.

There are two ways to construct steps. First, they can be built into sloping ground, so that the soil is shaped to be used as the foundations. Second, they can be completely freestanding where they are needed to take you not up or down a slope, but to a distinctly different level.

The prime consideration with the design is safety and you must ensure that users, especially the young and less active older people, feel comfortable on them. The flight must be neither too steep nor too narrow — both cases are dangerous because users are liable to trip or lose balance.

When planning garden steps it is important to keep the treads and risers uniform so that the walking rhythm is not broken.

The treads should be textured to make them non-slip – avoid smooth paving slabs or concrete, for example. After the steps have been built it is wise to check them regularly to ensure that moss or wet leaves are not left to form a potential skid-patch.

Where the land is steep and a long flight is needed you should design the steps so that there is a landing after about every ten steps. This gives a resting place for anyone feeling under strain. The landing can be in a straight flight or, very often, the steps can turn a corner at a landing for a more interesting visual effect.

A handrail is very useful, again

Above: brick steps, part inset and part freestanding, match the patio bricks.
Below: slate slabs form the treads here.

where young or less steady older people are around.

Where construction details are concerned, irrespective of the materials used, the following rules apply. The treads should be not less than 300mm (12in) from front to back and at least 600mm (2ft) wide. The front edge of each tread should project beyond the riser below by a distance of 25mm (1in).

The treads should fall very slightly towards the front so that rain water will drain quickly – a fall of about 8 to 10mm ($^5/_{16}$in to $^3/_8$in) is sufficient. Where the steps drop down towards the house, make a drainage gully.

The risers must be a minimum of 100mm (4in) and a maximum of 150mm (6in) high.

To give a comfortable rhythm to the steps, use long treads with low risers or short treads where you have high risers.

Inset steps

First fix two string lines running from the top to the bottom of the slope to indicate the overall width and length of the flight of steps. Now measure one string to find out the total length of the flight. From here you can calculate the number of steps there will have to be. You can then fix more string lines at right angles to the first two; these will represent the front edge of each step in the flight.

You can now shape the ground, starting at the bottom of the flight. The first riser has to be set on solid foundations, so dig a 125mm (5in) deep trench across the width of the flight. Place about 25mm (1in) of well compacted hardcore in the base and fill the remainder with concrete. Use a mix of one part cement to five parts ballast. Smooth this level with the ground surface.

If there is a lawn at the foot of the steps it is a good idea to lay a slab flush with the grass at the base of the steps to reduce wear and tear on the lawn.

Build the first brick riser on the concrete foundation or on the back of the first slab. Lay a bed of mortar about 100mm (4in) thick and build the tread level and square. Fill any gap between the back of the tread and the sloped earth with hardcore, and lay and compact a layer of hardcore on the first tread.

Now lay the paving slabs to form the tread. Again, bed these on mortar, ensuring that the front aligns with the string guide lines and that the tread projects 25mm.

The next riser is built on the back edge of the tread so that it has a good foundation. From then on the job is repetitive – back-filling each riser with hardcore, laying a layer of hardcore below the next tread and so on. For safety, the top tread must lie flush with ground level.

If the first step leads from a large paved area such as a terrace, on which water could collect, a drainage gully may be necessary to prevent the steps from becoming a dangerous waterfall in wet weather.

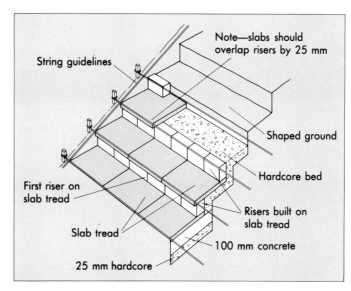

String guidelines
Note—slabs should overlap risers by 25 mm
Shaped ground
First riser on slab tread
Hardcore bed
Slab tread
Risers built on slab tread
100 mm concrete
25 mm hardcore

A cut-away drawing of inset steps in a slope. In this case the slabs of the first tread are flush with the lawn surface. The risers are built on the back of each tread and the space behind is filled with hardcore.

1 Dig out the steps, working from the bottom upwards. Allow for the thickness of the treads and risers.

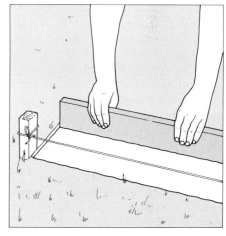

2 Lay a concrete bed for the first tread; allow for the covering slab to be flush with the lawn surface.

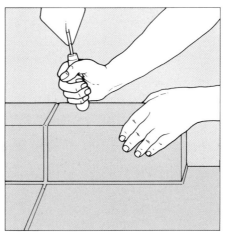

3 Build the risers on the backs of the treads, using bricks or stone walling blocks.

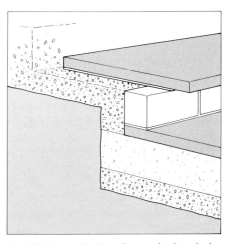

4 Fill in with hardcore behind the risers, then lay the treads on top on a layer of mortar.

Freestanding steps

Essentially, freestanding steps are constructed in exactly the same way as the previous type. The main difference is that your design options are far greater.

Remember that steps do not have to be built at right angles to the ground that they are leading down or up to. If space is at a premium, site them parallel with a terrace wall – a decided advantage where the change in levels is great.

The main extra work is in laying foundations for the walls, which must rise from the ground level to support all the treads from top to bottom of the flight.

If the flight consists of up to five steps then it is necessary only to dig foundations for the profile of the walls. Higher steps require a complete foundation below the construction. It is also necessary to anchor the walls of the steps into the terrace wall. This is achieved by taking out the appropriate bricks from the terrace wall to allow the last whole brick in alternate courses of the steps' walls to be built in.

First, set out the profile of the base of the steps using string guide lines. The concrete foundation trench should be double the thickness of the walls of the steps and 125mm (5in) deep. Insert 50mm (2in) of compacted hardcore topped with 75mm (3in) of concrete (one part cement to five parts ballast).

With two courses of the walls laid, allow time for the mortar to set and then fill the interior with the hardcore. Next, move the string line which denotes the front edge of the bottom step back to the position of the second riser so that this can be constructed. Continue in this way, resetting the strings to represent the next riser while it is built and then infilling with hardcore.

Check continually that the walls are being built vertically (see p 93). The final job is to lay the slabs for the treads, projecting them 25mm in front of the risers and sloping them slightly forward as well to ensure good drainage.

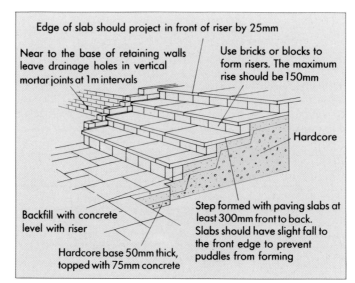

Edge of slab should project in front of riser by 25mm

Near to the base of retaining walls leave drainage holes in vertical mortar joints at 1m intervals

Use bricks or blocks to form risers. The maximum rise should be 150mm

Hardcore

Backfill with concrete level with riser

Step formed with paving slabs at least 300mm front to back. Slabs should have slight fall to the front edge to prevent puddles from forming

Hardcore base 50mm thick, topped with 75mm concrete

There are two ways to build freestanding steps. In this example, the steps are built between side walls. These are built first, then the steps are laid from the bottom upwards, like inset steps on the previous page. In the method below, for steps without side walls, the walls are built first, then the treads are laid.

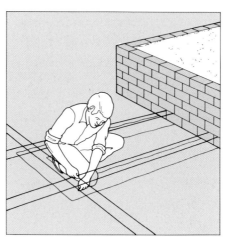

1 Cast foundations for the base of the steps and set out string lines for the walls.

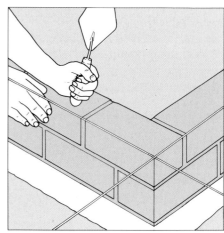

2 Build the walls around the shape of the steps up to the first tread height.

3 As you build the walls fill in the area behind with hardcore, surfaced with sand.

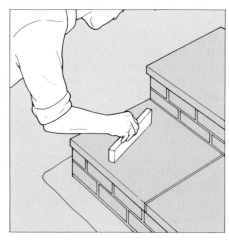

4 Finally, lay the tread slabs on mortar and tap them down to a slight forward fall.

Other types of step

It is important that steps blend comfortably into their surroundings. Obviously, where a patio has been laid with paving slabs or crazy paving, the same material should also be used for the treads of the steps. Bricks or reconstructed stone walling blocks are a natural choice for the side support walls or risers, especially when these materials have also been used on the patio, pathway, or wherever the steps lead. However, these are by no means the only choices for step building.

They might not be particularly attractive, but perfectly serviceable steps can be cast *in situ* from

Left: a steep flight of steps in weathered brick planned to blend pleasantly with the surroundings.

Below: rustic steps with log risers suit the woodland environment of this garden.

With rustic steps the risers can be timber or round logs to retain the treads which can be rubble surfaced with ballast. The risers can be held in place with timber pegs.

Log riser step

38–50 mm pole peg

Rubble surfaced with ballast

38 mm timber riser

38 × 38 mm timber peg

Right: the long flight of shallow steps has become an elegant feature of the garden.

concrete. You will need a lot of concrete, but the resulting steps will be very strong. Simple wooden shuttering, as you would make for a concrete foundation slab, will be required for a single step, while for a flight of steps you will need to build quite elaborate stepped shuttering using 19mm or 25mm (¾ or 1in) thick shuttering plywood braced with stakes.

For steps in a rustic setting – on a gravel path, for example – you can have 38mm (1½in) thick preservative-impregnated timber risers held in the sloping ground by pegs to retain the treads, which can be hardcore surfaced by rammed ballast.

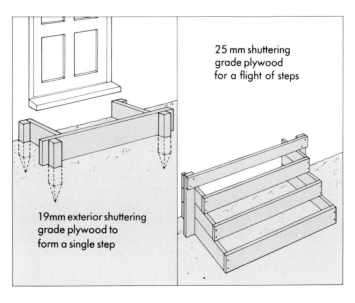

25 mm shuttering grade plywood for a flight of steps

19mm exterior shuttering grade plywood to form a single step

Concrete steps to be cast in situ need timber shuttering to retain the concrete while it sets. To reduce the amount of concrete required for a flight of steps, you can pack rubble into the space where the concrete would be thickest to leave a minimum concrete thickness of 125mm.

PONDS

By adding movement and sound to a garden, water has a way of bringing it to life. With a fountain, or waterfall, fish and plants, a garden pond brings both colour and year-round interest.

Important considerations are what type of pond it should be, how big, what shape, how it should be built, and where it should be sited. The last question is probably the most important; for the fish and plants to flourish you need an open site away from overhanging trees which not only cast shade, but fill the pond with leaves which then start to rot in the water. Ideally the pond should receive sunlight for at least half the day and be in a position where you can see it from the house.

The minimum surface area for a pond should be 4.5 sq m (48 sq ft). Depth should be at least 450mm (18in); a good average is 600mm (24in) and the maximum should be 750mm (30in). At the edge of the pond there should be a shelf 230mm (9in) deep on which you can grow marginal plants.

The shape should be simple and wide, such as a square, rectangle, circle or kidney-shape.

How the pool should be built depends on whether you want it in the ground, like a conventional pond, or whether you want a raised pool surrounded by low walls.

You can make a raised pool from the same materials as an in-ground one, but a good choice for the former is a rigid glassfibre moulded shape.

IN-GROUND POOL

Lay the liner on a base of damp sand and hide the edge with a surround of paving slabs

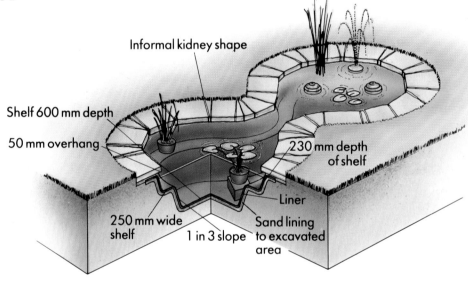

Informal kidney shape

Shelf 600 mm depth

50 mm overhang

230 mm depth of shelf

250 mm wide shelf

1 in 3 slope

Sand lining to excavated area

Liner

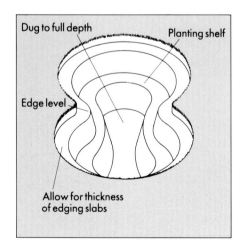

Dug to full depth

Planting shelf

Edge level

Allow for thickness of edging slabs

The excavated pool before the liner is positioned. Note that a shelf for marginal plants has been dug.

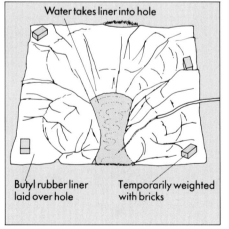

Water takes liner into hole

Butyl rubber liner laid over hole

Temporarily weighted with bricks

Position the liner over the hole and weight the edges with bricks. As the pool fills, lift them to ease pressure on the liner.

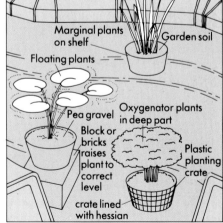

Marginal plants on shelf

Garden soil

Floating plants

Pea gravel

Oxygenator plants in deep part

Block or bricks raises plant to correct level

Plastic planting crate

crate lined with hessian

Set plants (other than floating varieties) in sacking-lined plastic crates, with pea gravel over the surface of the soil.

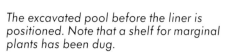

This type is self-supporting and you can simply stand them on the surface and surround them with walling to create an instant raised pond. The other type of moulded pool, the cheaper semi-rigid vacuum-formed type from weather-resistant plastic, needs careful support and protection from protruding stones and is best used for in-ground pools.

To install a rigid pool in the ground, excavate to leave the pool edges flush with the surrounding soil and with 150mm (6in) of extra space around the sides. Thoroughly compact the base and sides of the hole. Spread about 20mm (¾in) of damp sand over the base, insert the pond and check that the rim is level all round. Fill the cavity around the pond with damp sand, ramming it in place with a stick. To stop the pool moulding from lifting out of the hole, fill the pond with water as the sand is packed around its sides.

Flexible liners

Flexible liners are very popular for ponds because they give complete flexibility over shape and size. The best type, made of synthetic butyl rubber, should last for about 30 years; the next best, made of two layers of PVC reinforced with nylon net, should last for at least ten years.

To fit a liner, dig out the pond area to a depth of 230mm (9in) then dig out the central part to the depth required, leaving the 230mm (9in) deep by 250mm (10in) wide shelf around the perimeter. Compact the soil, remove any sharp stones and spread 20mm (¾in) of damp sand in the base. Lay the liner over the hole and fill it with water to stretch it into position. Trim off any surplus at the edges and finish neatly with paving stones.

Add plants a few days after filling the pond and add fish a month later.

RAISED POOL

A raised pool can be made with a flexible liner, as shown here, or with a moulded pool. With the latter type, a single brick wall will be sufficient.

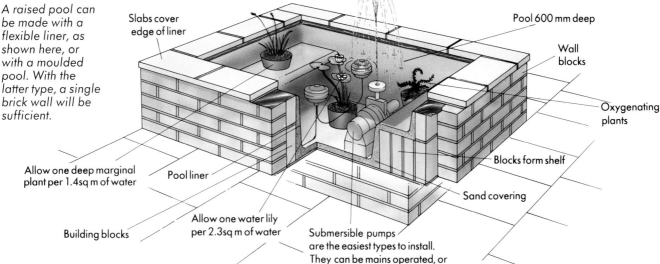

Slabs cover edge of liner

Pool 600 mm deep

Wall blocks

Oxygenating plants

Blocks form shelf

Sand covering

Allow one deep marginal plant per 1.4sq m of water

Pool liner

Building blocks

Allow one water lily per 2.3sq m of water

Submersible pumps are the easiest types to install. They can be mains operated, or supplied through a transformer.

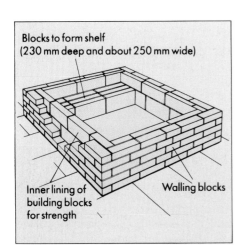

Blocks to form shelf (230 mm deep and about 250 mm wide)

Inner lining of building blocks for strength

Walling blocks

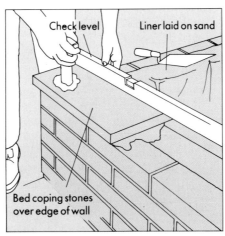

Check level

Liner laid on sand

Bed coping stones over edge of wall

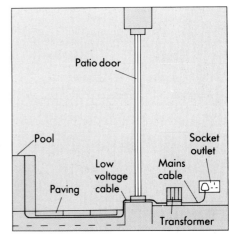

Patio door

Pool

Socket outlet

Low voltage cable

Mains cable

Paving

Transformer

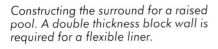

Constructing the surround for a raised pool. A double thickness block wall is required for a flexible liner.

After installing the flexible liner, trim the edges back to about 150mm (6in). Finish the top with coping stones on mortar.

For safety, lighting and a submersible pump can be worked from low-voltage transformers. Plug these in indoors.

PATIOS

When planning a new patio, the first thing to do is to work out exactly what you want from it. Will it be used mainly as an outdoor room when the weather is fine, with chairs and a table where you can sit and read, sunbathe, eat and entertain friends? If so, will you want to include a barbecue? Will the furniture be movable or will it be built-in as part of the patio?

Will you need space for children's games, so they have somewhere to play on days when the lawn is wet? Do you want to include a washing line, so you do not get muddy feet trudging down the garden on winter days?

Once you have established these preferences you can start envisaging exactly what sort of patio you want, in terms of both its size and its features.

Successful patios constructed from (above) hexagonal Derbyshire textured paving (left) old bricks, and (right) stone paving slabs. The design and material of a patio should fit the style of the house.

Choosing the best site is vital. The easiest is right next to the house but this is not always the best place. Perhaps the back of the house is in shade and it is at the bottom of the garden that the most sun and best shelter is available.

Do you need privacy? Screens can be made from planting, walls or fences to cut out prying eyes from overlooking windows.

Ideally the patio design should tie in with the style of the house – a very modern house needs a formal and modern arrangement; a cottage is suited to old brick and stone in an informal display; a Victorian villa will look happy with an ornamental design with plenty of plants, and a 1930s semi can look pleasant with either a formal arrangement of square paving or sweeping curves of crazy paving. Whichever style you use, make sure that you keep to the house materials as closely as possible – the same brick colour or stone paving colour.

Think about shape

A rectangle is an easy shape and does not need too much thought, but by making it slightly irregular it becomes far more interesting to look at. Even missing out one paving slab and filling the hole left with plants will give an instant change and visual excitement.

With careful planning on squared-up paper you can make adjustments and changes before you buy the materials. You can calculate more exactly, avoiding waste.

Use pegs and string to set out the proposed outline then see where you can improve it; check the shadows of

1 Lay the first slab at the intersection of the string lines.

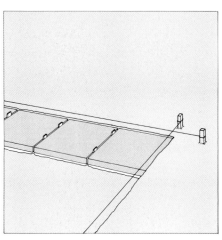

2 Use the lines as a guide to laying the perimeter slabs.

3 The mortar can be laid as five 'blobs', or a complete bed as here.

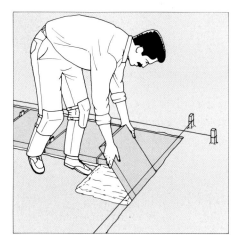

4 Lay each slab carefully on to the mortar bed.

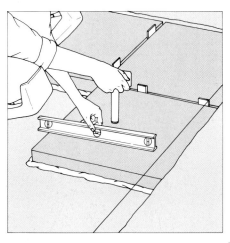

5 Check continuously for level and the correct fall.

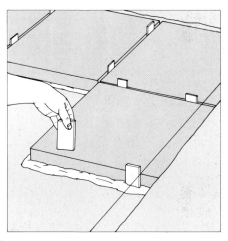

6 Spacers can be used to leave equal-size joints.

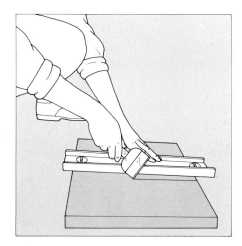

7 To cut a slab, first score on both faces.

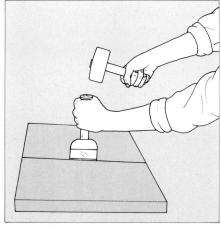

8 Use the bolster and club hammer to break the slab.

9 One way to fill joints is to brush in a dry sand and cement mix.

trees and buildings, angles of the sun, the position of the planting, and where the screening will be the most effective.

Patio materials

At this stage it is also a good idea to start thinking about the sort of materials you want to use for your patio.

Paving slabs are the most popular choice for patio surfaces. They are available in a wide range of types, shapes and sizes. There are squares and rectangles in a variety of sizes, colours and surface textures – including some very good imitations of natural York and Cotswold stone.

You can also buy interlocking hexagonal slabs, and even round stones that can be intermingled with materials such as cobbles. Laying is easy – either on a sand bed or on mortar over an existing concrete base – but larger slabs can be heavy to handle.

Looking for obstacles

Check any obstacles on the proposed site – for example, manholes (which can often be disguised), mature trees (which you may be able to make into a feature of the patio), even existing structures such as paths and clothes posts.

Foundations

The important part of any building project is the foundation. Provide a good base and you will have little to trouble you over the years. Skimp on the foundations and the patio will look rough and uneven, gradually getting worse as the ground settles and the weather takes its toll.

Sometimes a new patio area has to run across an existing concrete path or shed base. Where possible this should be broken up and used as hardcore but if it is really solid and thick then it is better to build over the top.

Never build over an air brick that ventilates the house floor or over the damp-proof course – allow for 150mm (6in) of space between the patio and the air bricks.

Always have a fall on the surface so that rainwater runs away from the house – 25mm (1in) in every 3m (10ft) is suitable.

Should paving be set into grass, or lie next to it, it should be slightly lower than the grass level to make mowing easy. Where there is grass next to a wall, cut back the turf for at least 100mm (4in) and lay a strip of concrete that also finishes below the level of the surface of the lawn.

A layer of hardcore will give you a substantial foundation that acts as a barrier between the soil and the paving. The mortar on which the slabs are bedded should be 1 part masonry cement to 4½ parts soft sand. The final consistency should be moist rather than wet and be easily worked.

Crazy paving

Randomly shaped stones present more design problems than straightforward paving slabs. Crazy paving is normally ordered by the ton or sq m/yd; if possible go and collect your own so that you can choose a good variety of large and smaller stones – and different colours, should you want them. You cannot devise an exact design before you start but it is best to work towards a good all-over mixture of colours, shapes and sizes. Lay the paving on the same foundations as standard paving. Use a full bed of mortar under each one (remember that the stones will not always be of equal thickness) and try to keep the joint spaces between the paving stones down to a maximum of 25mm (1in).

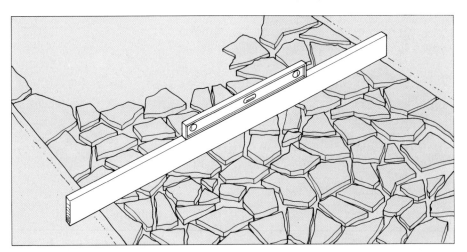

1 Use large, straight-sided pieces at the edges.

2 Check frequently with a spirit level as work proceeds.

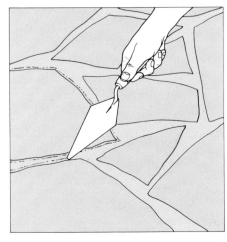

3 Use a trowel to etch the outline of each stone in the drying mortar.

EXTERIOR WALLS

Apart from maintaining the appearance of a house, sound walls help to prevent damp seeping through the masonry and spoiling decorations on the inside.

Walls are constructed of plain brickwork. This might be left exposed or covered by a layer of sand and cement mix (called rendering) or by pebble-dashing or roughcast. These finishes may or may not be painted with an exterior masonry paint.

Normally these repell damp, but problems can arise if defects develop or ageing causes the wall to become porous. If a damp patch is localized then you can be fairly certain that the fault is the cause and that an effective repair will cure the trouble.

If damp is getting through a sound wall, seal out the weather with a coat of good quality masonry paint or a colourless silicone water repellent.

Repointing brickwork

Use a cold chisel and club hammer to chip out crumbling mortar joints to a depth of 12mm (½in). Brush out all dust then dampen the joint with water. Repoint the joint, using a dryish mix of one part cement, one part hydrated lime, six parts soft sand; or use a ready-mix dry mortar.

Rendering

Cut out loose rendering. Dampen the wall and apply two layers of buttery render mix – one part cement, one part hydrated lime, six parts plastering sand. The first layer should come to within about 6mm (¼in) of the surface. Apply the second coat the following day.

Pebbledash and roughcast

Pebbledash is applied over two coats of rendering, using a small scoop or shovel. You have to paint the wall for the repair to be invisible. A hand-operated Tyrolean roughcast machine is used to splatter the mix onto the wall.

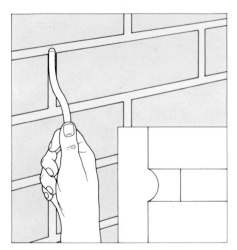

1 Draw a bucket handle through the drying mortar for a hollow joint.

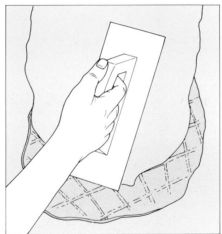

1 Score lines on the first layer of render to leave a key.

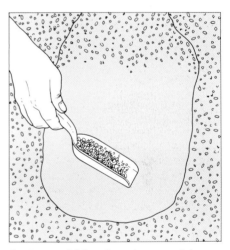

1 Any pebbles that do not stick can be pressed in with a wood float.

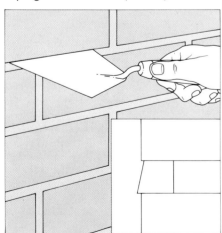

2 A pointing trowel drawn at an angle produces a weathered joint.

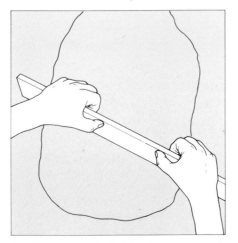

2 Draw a straight-edge upwards across the render to level it.

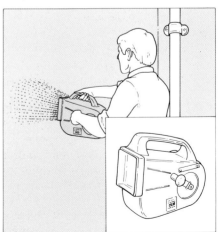

2 Turning the handle sprays the Tyrolean finish onto the wall.

FENCING

Fences come in many heights and designs. There are fences for privacy, fences for security, fences for boundary markers, fences to keep animals (and children) out, fences to keep children (and animals) in. You name it, and there is a fence to do it. It is just a question of picking the right type, and putting it up properly.

Closeboard fencing and ready-made panels provide instant security and are generally peep-proof, so it is natural that these are the ones usually considered first for domestic fencing.

They are easy to put up, require only a small amount of maintenance and will last for several years. If they do deteriorate or get damaged they are relatively easy to repair.

Boundary law If you are intending to erect a fence for the first time, remember that the law states that a boundary wall or fence which is more than 2m (6½ft) high (1m (3ft) if facing a road) will need planning permission.

Your first consideration in choosing a type of fence must be whether it will serve the purpose for which you intend it. Your budget will also be a consideration, but it is important too that the fencing you choose should be suited to its setting – a fence that looks wrong will fail to enhance the appearance and value of your house and could even make you unpopular with the neighbours. In some areas the planning authority's consent to the materials may be needed.

Planning is essential. Think carefuly about exactly where the fence is to go. Take measurements and look at any slopes and obstructions on the ground. Make a sketch plan of the layout, ideally working out where the post-holes must be dug. This will also help with estimating the quantity of materials.

Erecting a panel fence

Stretch a taut line along the pro-

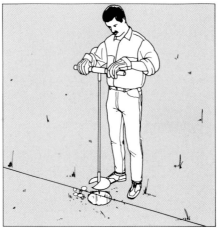

Three types of panel fence – overlap, interwoven, waney-edge

posed line of the fence. Whether using treated timber or concrete posts, for fences up to 1.2m (4ft) have about 450mm (18in) of post below ground; at least 600mm (2ft) for taller fences. The holes will have to be 150mm (6in) deeper than this to allow for hardcore at the bottom. You can dig the holes by hand, but if there are many of them it is well worth hiring a post-hole borer. Wedge broken bricks into the hole to keep the post upright.

If the fence butts up to a house wall, fix this post first, using expanding bolts.

Measure the position of the next post carefully then dig the next hole, insert the post and check it is in to the right depth by stretching a straightedge between adjoining posts and using a spirit level on top. Make sure the post is exactly in line with the string-line at the bottom. Use a spirit level to check that the

1 Stretch a string between pegs to show fence line.

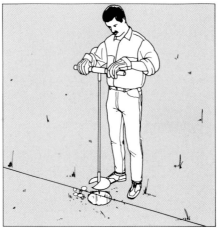

2 A post-hole borer makes it easier to dig holes.

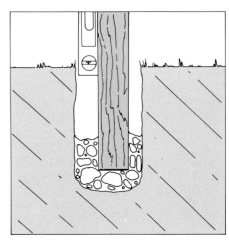

3 Place post in hole and support it with hardcore. Check for vertical.

posts are vertical.

If you are using concrete posts, the panels will simply slide in, but with timber posts you will need to nail the panels to the posts or use clips. Drill small holes for the nails so they do not split the wood – about three 75mm (3in) long galvanized nails on each side of the panel should be enough. Support the panel with blocks of wood if necessary before banging in the nails.

Make sure that the base of the panel is out of direct contact with the ground – if you do not want a gap, sit it on a row of bricks, or use a gravel board (a piece of timber at the bottom that can be replaced easily if it rots).

Use temporary struts to support the posts upright while the fence is being erected, and until the concrete has set firmly.

Posts for light fences offering little wind resistance can be held successfully with earth rammed tightly around them and with a few broken bricks wedged between the post and the edge of the hole.

If the fence is more substantial you will need to ram a dryish concrete mix of one part cement to four parts of ballast (mixed aggregate) into the hole, finishing with a sloping layer of concrete at the base of the post to drain water away from it. Leave the temporary supports in place for about four days.

Vertical closeboard

This is a solid, durable fence constructed with vertical overlapping boards nailed to two or three horizontal arris rails fixed between concrete or timber posts.

The boards are narrower at one edge than the other. The wide edge of one overlaps the narrow edge of its neighbour.

The triangular-section arris rails, which have squared ends, fit into slots in the posts.

Replaceable gravel boards run between the posts at ground level to prevent rot attacking the base of the vertical boards.

Right: the component parts of the typical vertical closeboard fence – traditional, familiar, and still one of the most widely used types.

Separate components are commonly available for assembly of the fence on site, although some pre-assembled panels are made.

If the fence is being built from parts, the posts (timber or concrete) are positioned every 2.4 or 3m (8 or 10ft) and need to be at least 100mm (4in) thick to allow for the weakening effect of the mortises for the arris rails. Two arris rails are needed for a fence 1.2m (4ft) high; three for a 1.8m (6ft) fence. Gravelboards are generally 200mm (8in) high and 25mm (1in) thick and the vertical boards 100 to 150mm (4 to 6in) wide.

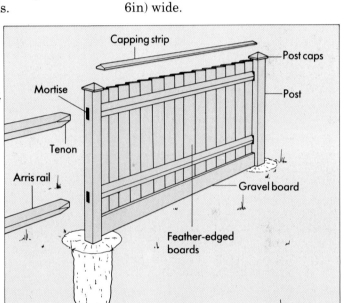

4 Use a length of wood equal to a panel to mark next hole position . . .

5 . . . or nail a panel to the post and support the free end on bricks.

6 The final job is to nail the post caps in position.

CARPORTS

A carport is a simple and cheap way of protecting a car. In some respects it is better than a garage because while the car is protected from the weather there is a good airflow under the canopy to dry off the car after it has been out in rain. One of the chief causes of vehicle corrosion is putting a wet car away in an unventilated garage.

A carport has other uses too. When the car is not there it is ideal as a clothes-drying area, and it makes an ideal place for children to play on wet days.

Probably you will not need planning permission or building regulations approval to erect a carport, but it is worth checking with your local planning authority at an early stage to find out if there are any special requirements.

A carport is basically a roof canopy on legs, which can be timber supports, steel struts, or brick piers. There are lots of ways of going about the job, but the end result must be a structure that is waterproof, wind-resistant, and capable of withstanding the loading of snowfall.

Choosing materials

Carports are available in kit form, usually consisting of a metal framework clad in clear plastic roofing sheets. If you are making a carport

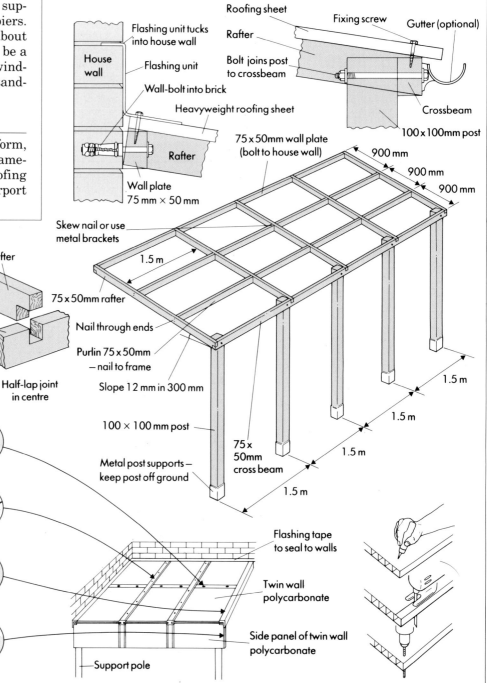

Roofing sheet
Fixing screw
Gutter (optional)
Flashing unit tucks into house wall
Rafter
House wall
Flashing unit
Bolt joins post to crossbeam
Wall-bolt into brick
Heavyweight roofing sheet
Crossbeam
100 x 100mm post
Wall plate 75 mm × 50 mm
Rafter
75 x 50mm wall plate (bolt to house wall)
900 mm
900 mm
900 mm
Skew nail or use metal brackets
1.5 m
75 x 50mm rafter
Nail through ends
Purlin 75 x 50mm — nail to frame
Slope 12 mm in 300 mm
100 × 100 mm post
Metal post supports — keep post off ground
75 x 50mm cross beam
1.5 m
1.5 m
1.5 m
1.5 m
1.5 m

Crossbeam
Rafter
Half-lap joint at corner

Rafter
Crossbeam
Half-lap joint in centre

Fixing buttons to secure cross purlins

Glazing bars where sheets join

'F' profile on outside edges

'U' profile on top and bottom edges

Flashing tape to seal to walls

Twin wall polycarbonate

Side panel of twin wall polycarbonate

Support pole

from scratch it will probably be best to make the roof structure from a timber frame which is clad in plastic roofing sheets. On one side the carport will probably be supported by a timber beam, called a wallplate, bolted to a building. The other side of the roof is supported by legs and it will probably be best to make these from timber. Galvanized steel tubing is ideal for the purpose, but this is harder to work than timber and it is more difficult to attach the steel supports to the roof members. Brick piers are sturdy supports, but building piers calls for considerable bricklaying skills.

A carport should be built with a good overhang to protect the car parked under it from driving rain. If you have the space, 2.4m (8ft) is a good minimum width for a carport, and a good length to aim for is 6m (20ft).

Roofing

The roof cladding can be 10mm-thick twin-wall polycarbonate, which is extremely strong, lightweight and shatterproof. It is also expensive, and a cheaper alternative for roofing where shatter-resistance is not so important is corrugated PVC sheets. These are available with conventional round or box-section 75mm (3in) profiles. For a large structure such as a carport it is best to use the heavyweight grades of these roofing sheets.

With corrugated PVC sheets it does not matter what width you build your carport because the sheets can be overlapped end to end (unlike twin-wall polycarbonate where you are limited to the length of sheet available) and overlapped side to side to cover any area.

For heavy-duty PVC, design the supporting timber framework so that the corrugated sheets have cross supports (purlins) at about 900mm (36in) intervals along their length. The purlins can be cut from 75 × 50mm (3 × 2in) sawn timber.

Nail the purlins to a timber frame which is also made from 75 × 50mm sawn timber and comprises rafters joined using half-lap joints to an outer crossbeam and wallplate. Butt-join the purlins into the rafters by simply nailing them in place or fixing them with metal brackets. The wallplate is bolted to the wall using expanding wall-bolts.

Away from the house wall, support the carport roof on preservative-treated 100 × 100mm (4 × 4in) timber posts bolted at the top to the roof cross-beam. At the base screw them to proprietary metal post supports (they may need trimming to fit) which are driven into the ground or set in the concrete base. Alternatively, set galvanized steel posts in the base concrete at the required post positions. Use a spirit level to check that the posts are vertical before the concrete sets. At the top the posts can be drilled for bolting directly to the timber roof frame. Drill the posts after they have been positioned to ensure that the frame is level.

Fit the posts so they are about 1.5m (5ft) apart. They should be long enough to give adequate headroom (2.3m [7ft 6in] minimum). Cut them to give a slope on the roof of 12mm in 300mm (½in in 12in).

Sheets should have a 1½-ridge overlap against adjacent sheets at the side; if it is necessary to overlap sheets endways allow a 150mm (6in) overlap. Use clear sealing tape to seal lengthways joins, and seal joins across sheets with clear silicone rubber mastic. Fix sheets with screws and washers inserted through pre-drilled holes in the top of the corrugations. Drill every third ridge.

Covered ways

Making a covered way is just like making a mini-carport. However, in this case shatter-resistance could be an important requirement, so it may be necessary to roof-in the structure with twin-wall polycarbonate. While 10mm-thick sheet will give the strongest job, 6mm or 8mm-thick sheet will be adequate for a covered way where the span is unlikely to exceed 1.2m (4ft), and this will result in a significant cost saving. You will require supports of 75 × 50mm (3 × 2in) at the edges of the sheets (widths vary according to the thickness of the sheet chosen). Use glazing bars, screwed to the timber supports, to join the sheets side by side, and to fix them down. Special plastic bars are available to seal the sheets at the sides and ends.

Above: a climbing plant has made an attractive feature of this simple carport.

CONCRETE

Provided that it is properly mixed and laid on a firm foundation, a concrete path, drive or base will last a lifetime. Concrete is both simple to make and use, though it can be tough going for anyone not accustomed to manual work. It is a good idea to enlist the help of a friend or two for large projects; alternatively, tackling the job in short stages is a perfectly acceptable way of working. It is best not to work in extreme temperatures – a boiling hot day will add to the toil and a freezing winter's day can lead to cracks developing later on in your new path or drive.

Concrete is made by mixing Portland cement with aggregate, which is more commonly called ballast.

Bags of cement should be stored under cover and on a platform of boards or bricks so that they are clear of the ground.

For all general-purpose jobs, a mix of one part cement to four parts ballast (by volume) is suitable. For footings, foundations and bases for precast paving, use one part cement to five parts ballast.

To find the volume of concrete required in cubic metres, multiply the length (in m), the width (in m) and the thickness (in mm) and divide by 1,000. Now refer to the table opposite for quantities of cement and ballast to order.

Volume (m^3)	0.5	1	2	3	4	5
1:4 mix:						
Cement (50 kg bags)	3½	7	14	21	28	35
Ballast (m^3)	0.5	1	2	3	4	5
1:5 mix						
Cement (50kg bags)	3	6	12	18	24	30
Ballast (m^3)	0.5	1	2	3	4	5

Tools and equipment

Buckets – two same-size buckets are needed. Keep one solely for the cement, the other for ballast and water. Same-size buckets make it easy to keep the ingredients in their correct proportions when adding to the mix.

Shovels – two. Keep one solely for cement.

Wheelbarrow – used for transporting loads of mixed cement to the site. Make sure it is a sturdy type; a lightweight one used normally for collecting garden weeds is not suitable.

Steel float – for smooth finishing the concrete.

Wood float – for a textured finish.

Tamper – used to compact the concrete. For small widths and thin sections, a piece of 100 × 50mm (4 × 2in) timber will suffice. For wider areas or thicker slabs, a 150 × 50mm (6× 2in) timber is better. The tamper will be easier to use if it is fitted with handles. The tamper should be about 30cm (12in) wider than the framework.

Garden roller – for compacting the base.

Rake – for spreading concrete inside formwork.

For setting out site and formwork – saw, hammer, tape measure, spirit level, straightedge, hosepipe, builder's square, string, pegs.

Choosing and mixing

There are four ways of making concrete materials. The one chosen will depend on cost, convenience, the size and position of the work area, and whether the job is to be completed as quickly as possible or be spread over a period of weeks. Another consideration is the method of mixing.

Hand mixing – by far the hardest way but also the most economical. You order the separate ingredients and mix them up in batches to suit your working speed. Should the work have to be spread over several evenings, mixing small batches at a time, then this is a good method.

Dry mixes – small bags of dry mixed cement and ballast to which water is added. Economy rules out this type for larger jobs such as path laying. However, they are viable for smaller areas or repair work.

Machine mixing – here you order the cement and ballast then hire or borrow a cement mixer and let that do the mixing.

Ready-mixed – Order the amount of concrete you require. It has to be laid within a couple of hours of delivery – less on a really hot day – so everything must be prepared in advance.

Should it be possible for the lorry to drop the concrete direct into the formwork, so much the better. If the concrete has to be shunted to the worksite in wheelbarrows, a small army of helpers should be standing by at the ready.

Preparing the site

Clear any weeds, grass or other vegetation (including roots), then compact the soil.

Fill soft spots with hardcore and again roll to make firm. The new concrete path or drive will now stand proud of the surrounding terrain. Should you want it to lie flush, the complete site will have to be dug out to the intended thickness of the concrete.

Hardcore should be laid on soft ground. The hardcore base plus the thickness of the concrete will give the finished level of the concrete. A 50mm (2in) layer of hardcore plus 50mm (2in) of concrete will suit a path. Increase the hardcore and concrete to 75mm (3in) for a drive or shed base.

1 Drive pegs into the ground to the correct height for the formwork and set them level with a spirit level.

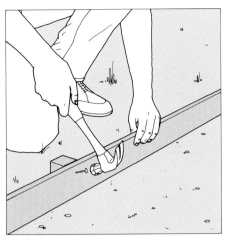

2 Check that the boards are horizontal then nail them to the pegs, flush with the peg tops.

3 Ensure that both sides of the formwork are level. On wider slabs use extra pegs as a guide.

4 To bend formwork for a curved path make saw cuts to half the timber depth.

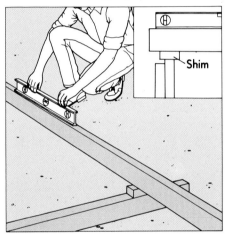

5 When a cross fall is needed use a shim on one side of the formwork to set the level.

6 For a shed base use a builder's square to check that all corners are at right angles.

Marking out the site

Paths Knock pegs into the ground at the start and finishing points on both sides of the path. Use lengths of string, pulled taut and tied to the pegs, to indicate the two sides of the path. The string lines are the guide to the position of the timber formwork.

Use lengths of timber for the formwork. Old floorboards or fence boards are ideal. The timbers should be the same height as the desired thickness of the concrete. Thus, if a 7.5cm (3in) thick path is being laid, the timbers must be 7.5cm (3in) high. To support the timbers, drive timber pegs into the ground every few feet and nail the formwork to the pegs.

To ensure rainwater drainage, the path will need a slight crossfall. For a 1m (3ft) wide path, a fall of 12mm (½in) is sufficient. To arrange this, position a 12mm (½in) thick piece of timber (called a shim) on one side of the formwork and place a straight-edge across the formwork so that one side rests on the 12mm (½in) shim. Place a spirit level on the straight-edge and knock down the section of formwork with the shim resting on it until a level reading is recorded on the spirit level. A fall of 12mm (½in) in 1m (3ft) will now exist at this point across the path. The operation must be repeated at several points.

For a curved path the timber formwork can be bent to shape if a series of sawcuts is made to half the depth of the timber.

If you are laying a path against a wall, use the arrangement shown above. The alternate bay sequence allows you to compact the concrete in alternate bays by standing in the vacant bays. Complete these when the concrete in the adjoining bays has cured.

You could lay a narrower path in one sweep by kneeling outside the formwork.

Remember that the finished level of a path laid against a house wall

7 Lay hardcore in the base of the site and compact it with a heavy timber or roller.

8 Pour the concrete into a corner to start. Spread it out with a rake so it is just above the formwork.

9 Use the tamping beam in an up-and-down movement to level the concrete.

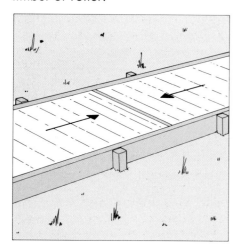

12 Lay the next bay in the opposite direction, working up to the support board. Remove, and fill the gap.

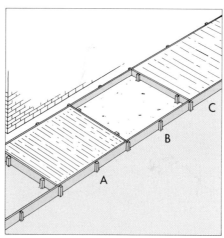

13 If concreting against a wall use the alternate bay method. When A and C are hard, concrete bay B.

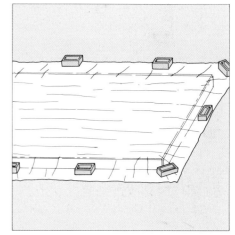

14 Cover the fresh concrete with thick plastic weighted down at the edges.

should be at least 150mm (6in) below the house damp-proof course. Also there should be a crossfall built in to ensure that rainwater runs away from the wall.

Bases A simple rectangular base is shown here. For this job a builder's square is needed. You can make one by joining three lengths of wood together with its sides being in the proportions of 3:4:5. The most convenient size is 45 × 60 × 75cm (18 × 24 × 30in). The angle between the shortest sides will be 90°. A crossfall is not needed for a shed or greenhouse base. Check the formwork in all directions with a spirit level to establish an all-over level.

Mixing by hand

A uniform mix is important, so measure out the correct number of buckets of ballast into a pile, then make a depression in the top of the pile and add the cement. For a 1:5 mix you would use one bucket of cement and five buckets of ballast.

Turn over the pile with the shovel until a uniform colour is obtained. Make a further depression and add about half the water. You will need about half a bucket of water for each bucket of cement.

Add the water gradually, turning over the pile until it is well mixed – aim for an even colour and consistency. It should be a little dry and

crumbly. Add the remainder of the water into a newly formed depression and continue mixing.

When the concrete seems usable, tread on it a couple of times; if water runs out readily the mixture is too weak and more mixing is required, or too much water has been added. If the latter seems the case, add a tiny amount of cement and aggregate and mix again.

Dry mix bags

Do not just pour these on to the ground and add water. The ingredients will have tended to separate in the bag, so mix them up first to get a consistent overall colour.

10 Next pull the beam back and forth using a sawing movement to reveal any low spots.

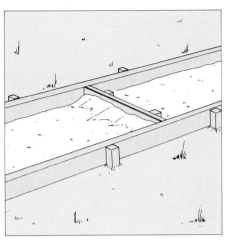

11 When making a joint, concrete up to the joint board on the side of the hardboard.

15 A soft broom gives a smooth finish, a stiff bass broom leaves a deeper texture.

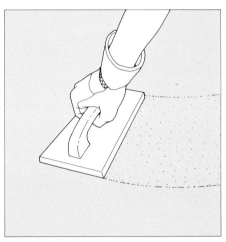

16 A wood float used in sweeping curves will produce a non-slip sandpaper surface.

Machine mixing

Shovel in half the aggregate and water; let them spin round for 30 seconds or so before adding all the cement, then the remainder of the ballast and water. Allow a final mixing period of about three minutes.

Laying the concrete

Pour the concrete into the formwork; use the back of a rake to bring it level, slightly proud of the top edges of the timbers. At all corners and edges, press the concrete well down to make sure all cavities are filled.

Each batch must be compacted with a tamper as it is spread. Rest the tamper on the edge of the form-work, then use it in a chopping motion, moving it along about half the thickness of the board each time it is dropped. This will create an undulating effect. Go over the high spots, using the tamper in a sawing motion. Fill depressions with scoopfuls of concrete. Aim for an all-over level surface. Make a final sweep using the tamper.

Finishes

Tamped finish. Suitable for a garage drive – stop after the final chopping pass with the tamper. If the final pass is with a sawing motion, a rippled effect will result.
Brushed finish. Use a soft broom for a smoother finish. Brushing will produce different textures, depending on how far the concrete has set.

For a deeper brushed finished, use a stiff bass broom over the fresh concrete.
Wood float. Use with a semi-circular movement to produce a non-slip 'sandpaper' finish.
Steel float. After the wood float treatment, allow the concrete to stiffen. Before it has set completely, use the steel float in a semi-circular for a smooth surface.

Protection

Concrete must not dry out too quickly. If it does it will be weak. In warm weather allow the concrete to harden sufficiently so that it will not be affected by a covering material.

Use plastic sheeting as a covering and weight down the edges. Hessian or sacking can be used, but it must be kept constantly damp for about two or three days.

Joints in the concrete

To prevent concrete cracking, expansion joints must be inserted in slabs of a certain size. A joint is made by placing a piece of hardboard in the concrete and supporting it with a piece of 12mm (½in) softwood and pegs.

A 7.5cm (3in) thick base for a shed or greenhouse can be a complete slab provided that the longest dimension is no more than 3m (10ft) and the length is no more than twice the width. Areas outside these stipulations should be divided into two or more slabs with joints between them. The bays should be as square as possible and equal in size.

In a path, joints should be at 2 to 2.5m (6½ to 8ft) spaces. The narrower the path, the closer the joints. In a drive, the joints should be at intervals of about 3m (10ft).

Concrete right up to the hardboard joint board. In the next bay, fill to within a few inches of the support board and pegs. Remobe the 12mm (½in) support board and pegs and fill up to the joint board. The joint board remains in the concrete.

BRICKWORK

Bricklaying requires taking care and having confidence. Learn both aspects on a small project. Practise first by taking a few bricks into the garden and laying a couple of courses on a flat piece of ground – a sheet of plywood laid on the patio is ideal. Build up the wall, then knock it down. Clean the mortar from the bricks before it dries and have another go. In no time you will be able to judge how much mortar to spread as a bed for a brick.

At first you should check the whole wall generally and each brick after it is laid. It is simple to re-lay a single brick, but time-consuming and disappointing to have to knock down a couple of courses.

For most garden projects choose ordinary quality solid facing bricks, in a colour and texture you like or which blend in with the brickwork of your house. If you are building retaining walls or brick steps, upgrade the specification to special quality. It is important to remember to leave drainage holes in earth-retaining walls.

Bricks are made to a standard size:– 215mm (8½in) long, 102.5mm (4in) wide and 65mm (2½in) high. However, for the purpose of estimating quantities, allowance is made for a 10mm (½in) thick mortar joint all round; this gives what is known as the format size of 225 × 112.5 × 75mm (9 × 4½ × 3in). When designing your wall, try to work to complete brick dimensions.

Preparing the site

Set up profile boards at each end of the site, well back from the ends of the concrete foundation trench. Cut notches in the top edge of each board and stretch string lines between them to represent the thickness of the wall and the width of the trench. The string lines for the wall should be fixed when the trench is completed.

Dig the trench and drive timber pegs into the bottom. The tops of the pegs must be at the proposed surface-level of the concrete and should therefore be made level with a timber straightedge and a spirit level. Lay the concrete, compact it thoroughly and allow it to harden for at least four days before starting to build the wall.

Bonds

The way the bricks are bonded gives a wall its strength. The vertical joints between bricks in adjacent courses must not coincide either on the face of the wall or across its thickness. Some examples of bonding arrangements are shown above. A half-brick wall up to 1m (3ft) high can be built in stretcher or open bond. You should bond in piers of 328 × 215mm (13 × 8½in) at the ends of the wall and at a maximum of 1.8m (6ft) centres. A 215mm (8½in) wall can be built using English or Flemish bond. Careful cutting is needed at junctions and

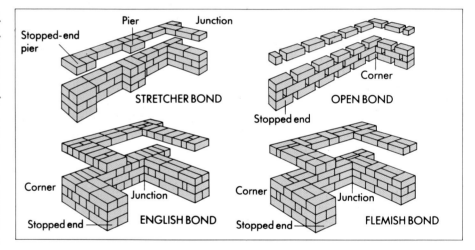

corners to avoid continuous vertical joints through two or more courses.

Mortar

Bricks are bonded together with mortar, which is a mixture of cement, soft builder's sand, lime or plasticizer (to improve workability) and water. You can either buy the ingredients separately or purchase bags of dry ready-mixed mortar. The latter are fine for really small projects (or for your first practice session) but will work out very expensive on larger jobs, for which you really need separate ingredients.

Cement is sold in 50kg bags. Ordinary Portland cement is used for most jobs, but you can buy white Portland cement if you are using pale bricks. Sand is sold by the cubic metre. Small quantities may be sold bagged, while larger amounts will be delivered loose. It is also sold in 50kg bags. Lime comes in bags of various sizes, but you may prefer to use a liquid plasticizer instead (you add this to the water when mixing up your mortar); alternatively, buy masonry cement which already contains a plasticizer.

The mix to use for general-purpose bricklaying is 1:1:5 cement: lime:sand, measured by volume. As a guide to estimating mortar quantities, one bag of cement plus 0.2 cubic metres of damp sand will make enough mortar to lay about 400 bricks. A 50kg bag of dry ready-mixed mortar will be enough to lay around 60 bricks.

Mix mortar on a clean, flat surface and use two equal size buckets for measuring, one solely for cement.

Mix all the ingredients dry, then form a crater in the centre of the heap and add some water. Mix in the mortar from the sides of the heap, turning it thoroughly, and add more water as necessary until the consistency is firm enough to form smooth ridges when the spade is drawn across the heap with a chopping motion. Do not mix up too much at once – no more than you can use in an hour – especially on a hot day.

Foundations

A firm, level base that will prevent the wall from subsiding or collapsing is essential. You can build simple structures, such as brick planters, on an existing sound path, patio or drive, but anything else needs proper concrete foundations.

For a garden wall or similar structure, lay a strip of concrete in the ground. As a general guide, for a small wall up to 1m (3ft) high the following can be applied. For a 215mm (8½in) thick wall (two skins of brick) lay 230mm (9in) of concrete in a 500mm (19½in) wide trench at least 500mm (19½in) below ground level. For a half-brick (single skin of brick) lay 150mm (6in) of concrete in a 300mm (12in) wide trench, 350 to 400mm (14–16in) below ground level. The concrete for foundations should be a mix of one part cement to five parts ballast.

Allow the foundations to harden for at least four days before starting to lay bricks and cover it with polythene if rain threatens, or damp sacking if the sun is hot. Do not lay concrete in frosty weather.

Laying bricks

The first course of bricks is very important. Bed the first brick on a level layer of mortar, spread with the trowel. Lay a second brick a few feet along the string line and bridge the two bricks with a straightedge. Place the spirit level on the straightedge and make any adjustments to the higher brick to bring the two level. If the bricks have an indentation in them (called a frog) this is always faced upwards.

1 Set up profile boards and string lines at either end of the trench. Dig the trench and lay foundations.

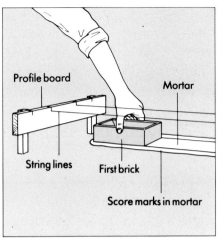

2 Position the first brick accurately on mortar laid between the string guide lines.

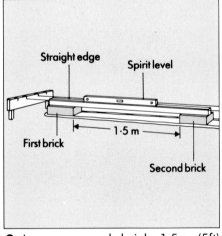

3 Lay a second brick 1.5m (5ft) away and check that the two bricks are level.

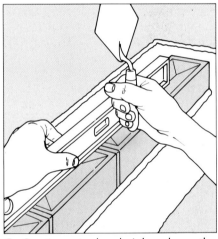

4 Continue to lay bricks along the first course, checking each one carefully.

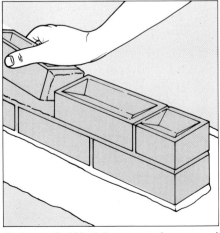

5 Lay a half brick to start the second course, then continue as before.

6 As the wall builds up, check continuously that the bricks are plumb.

7 A gauge stick, marked off in brick courses, is used to check that all joints are even.

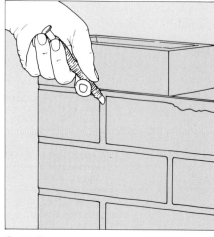

8 Follow a string guide line as the wall is built. Stretch it between pins driven into the mortar joints.

9 Build up the ends of the wall first, then fill in with bricks between, one course at a time.

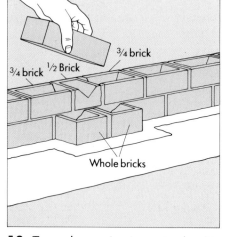

10 To make a pier in a single skin wall, use the bonding arrangement shown.

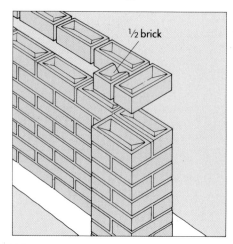

11 To finish off the ends of the wall use this bonding arrangement of half and whole bricks.

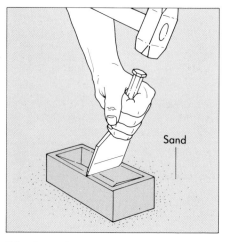

12 Cut a brick by laying it on sand; score all round then cut through using a bolster and club hammer.

The mortar should be a little thicker than 10mm (½in) to allow for compression.

Lay a band of mortar about 300mm (12in) long for each brick. Butter a 10mm (½in) layer of mortar on the end of each brick before laying it. To tap down a brick, use the handle of the trowel.

Continue as above until the first course of bricks is laid completely. Each joint in the course should then be pointed (see joint finishes).

The corners of the wall must be built up so that the corners are stepped up to four courses above the one being worked on.

Stretch a bricklayer's line between the corners of the next course before the bricks are laid. Make sure that all the corners bricks are plumbed truly vertically. Check each complete course with a gauge rod, and for vertical with the spirit level.

On a hot day, wet the bricks before laying them.

The top of the wall requires a coping course. For a half-brick wall, standing a brick on edge is sufficient. These, if you prefer, can be cut in half to stand on edge. A neat finish to a 225mm (9in) wall is a whole brick standing on edge. Coping bricks should be the dense type – not ordinary flettons: they are to protect the wall from the elements.

Joint finishes

Flush joints are made simply by scraping away any excess mortar using the edge of the pointing trowel to leave the joints flush with the face of the brick.

Weathered joints are the most difficult to make. Fill the cavity with mortar, leaving it slightly proud of the surface. The aim is to wipe the trowel at an angle along the joint. To complete the horizontal joints, slope the mortar out towards the bottom edge by pressing inwards with the top edge of the trowel.

A half-round length of metal is used for round joints. This bar is pressed along the joint to leave a smooth, concave band of mortar.

INDEX